what people are saying about

HULLABALOO

If you've ever felt disappointed with God or overwhelmed by the pressures of life, Hullabaloo *is for you! Timothy Paul Jones has struggled with both. Yet he refuses to wallow in life's disappointments or to gloss over its pressures with naive clichés. Unlike many authors, Jones also refuses to reduce the solutions to life's complex difficulties to one more to-do list. Instead, he wrestles creatively with the complexities of life and arrives at a surprising conclusion: Everything you need to live a life of glory is already available in the life that you're presently living. He then shows readers how to drink deeply from the glory that God has already placed within them. A fresh perspective on the age-old struggle to rely completely on what God has accomplished in Jesus Christ!*

—*Dr. Jim Garlow, senior pastor, Skyline Church, San Diego*

The glory-insights discovered in Hullabaloo *brought clarity to my eyes of faith, making me more aware of God's glorious presence in each day of life. As always, Timothy Paul Jones' conversational and personal writing style make for a most enjoyable read—and a glorious blessing!*

—*Tim Wesemann, best-selling author,* Jack Bauer's Having a Bad Day: An Unauthorized Investigation of Faith in 24: Season One

In a world full of "uproar and fuss" where everything in life seems to run together, Jones takes "learning the art of life" and elevates it to the glorious and reduces it to the practical at the same time. He challenges the reader to address the hunger within, to wrestle with what the really glorious things in life are, and to realize that the glorious is found where you least expect it. Then, he challenges the reader to find some creative way to get rid of this book. Jones deals with questions that arise from the collisions that occur at the intersection of faith and life, and helps the reader to rise above the hullabaloo.

—DANIEL J. GRIMES
30 YEAR PASTOR; ASSOCIATE PROFESSOR OF CHURCH MINISTRIES AT ORAL ROBERTS UNIVERSITY

From the introduction's poignant story of two young Puerto Rican girls to the jarring "Get Rid of This Book" title of the afterword, Jones' captivating writing style will inform and enlarge your perception of glory forever. An engaging book for individuals and small groups alike to read. It will result in a hullabaloo in your soul.

—SCOTTIE MAY, WHEATON COLLEGE

Do you still stink at following Jesus? I do. And the cool thing about Dr. Timothy Paul Jones' book is that even though he's all degreed up with doctorates and a seminary man of papers, he still dines on humble pie and writes, sure enough, very personally, out of his own hullabaloo while pastoring First Baptist Church of Rolling Hills. This book tells of his journey to see God's glory in spite of and perhaps because of his own failures and a few bright moments as a dad and husband, pastor, and normal guy. The book's full of great stories that are not calculated to make Jones look like a hero but like one of us who is learning, like you and me, to follow Jesus 24/7/365, except leap year when it's one day extra. Do yourself and a friend a favor and buy two copies, read it together, and perhaps you'll discover together that you can't control life's hullabaloo around you, but you can learn to see God's glory much more often than Sundays and Wednesday nights.

—GREG TAYLOR, MANAGING EDITOR, WWW.WINESKINS.ORG; ASSOCIATE MINISTER, GARNETT CHURCH OF CHRIST, TULSA, OKLAHOMA

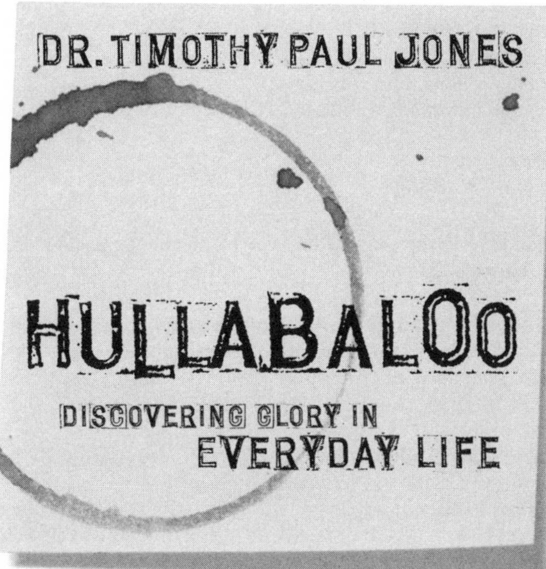

Bringing Home the Message for Life

COOK COMMUNICATIONS MINISTRIES
Colorado Springs, Colorado • Paris, Ontario
KINGSWAY COMMUNICATIONS LTD
Eastbourne, England

Life Journey® is an imprint of
Cook Communications Ministries, Colorado Springs, CO 80918
Cook Communications, Paris, Ontario
Kingsway Communications, Eastbourne, England

Timothy Paul Jones is represented by Mike Nappa at Nappaland Literary Agency, http://www.nappaland.com.

Cover Design: studiogearbox.com
Cover Image: Steve Gardner/PixelWorks Studios
Interior Design: Karen Athen

First Printing, 2007
Printed in the United States of America

1 2 3 4 5 6 7 8 9 10

ISBN 978-0-7814-4483-5
LCCN 2007929487
052907

To

the glorious people of God

who gather each week

at

First Baptist Church of

Rolling Hills,

especially

my most faithful readers

Deby Nottingham

and

Laura Franklin

I learned to see

the glory in my life's hullabaloo

through the splendor and the sorrow

that I shared in this place with you.

I HAVE A FEELING THAT MY BOAT HAS STRUCK, DOWN THERE IN THE DEPTHS, AGAINST A GREAT THING. AND NOTHING HAPPENS! ... NOTHING HAPPENS? OR HAS EVERYTHING HAPPENED AND ARE WE STANDING NOW, QUIETLY, IN THE NEW LIFE?

—JUAN RAMÓN JIMÉNEZ, "OCEANS"

CONTENTS

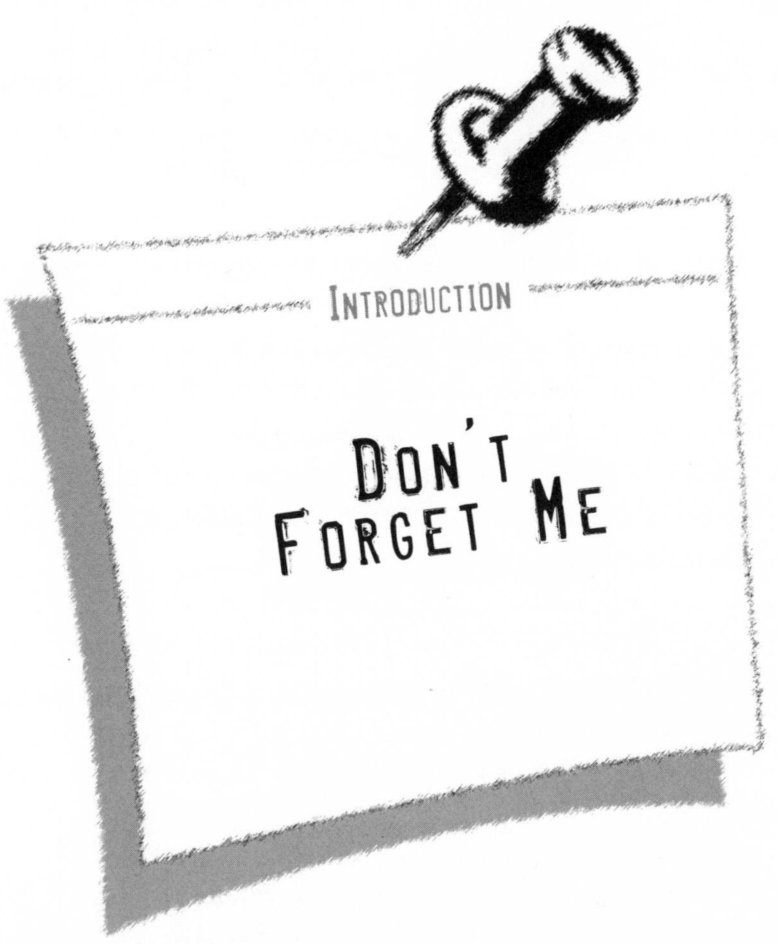

Introduction

Don't Forget Me

> In the middle of our life's way,
> I found myself in a wood so dark that
> I could not tell where the straight path lay.
>
> —Dante Alighieri, *The Inferno*

A few years ago, I found myself struggling through a wood that was, I'm quite certain, at least as dark as Dante's. I would like to think that I have yet to reach the midpoint of my life, but I cannot be certain; this forest provided no window into worlds to come. This wood was a deep, inner barrenness in which something my soul deeply craved seemed to have slipped from my grasp—something elusive yet infinitely meaningful and true, something that filled life with beauty and splendor.

The word that I've chosen to describe this "something" is *glory*.

When I use the word *glory*—as I will many times in this book—I am simply referring to the awareness that God is fully available in every present moment of my life. It's the inward knowledge that God is closer than I ever imagined and that there is no presence in heaven or on earth that matters more. It's the persistent recognition that every molecule of space and every moment of time are swollen to the point of bursting with the splendor of God.

I find it interesting that the root meaning of the word translated *glory* in Hebrew is weightiness. This image perturbed me for a while. After I first noticed this phenomenon, every time I read about "the glory of God," I envisioned an obese old man on a throne, sort of an elderly version of the laughing Buddha. I didn't mean to think of God in this way; that's just the image that kept charging through my mind.

So I did some research and discovered that this etymological oddity most likely stems from the fact that, if something really mattered to ancient civilizations, it was crafted from heavy materials. The most valuable monuments weren't crafted from wood or leaves; they were carved in stone, silver, or gold. As a result, to describe something as "weighty" or "glorious" was to recognize that it had extreme—even infinite—value.[1]

This facet of the word *glory* has profound implications for the way I look at my life. For example, if God is present in every moment of my life and if every object is surrounded by his glory, every event of my life and everything in it is infinitely valuable. Here and now, my life is filled with infinite glory.

It's the same with your life too, you know.

Here and now, infinite glory surrounds you.

And yet, there are times when I lose sight of the eternal glory that fills every minute of my life. In place of glory, I find only the hubbub and hullabaloo of ordinary existence—the constant, soul-numbing emptiness of a world that will not slow down, a dulling rhythm of busyness pierced occasionally by a moment of pleasure or pain.

You've felt it too—that sense of emptiness in the exact places where you long to feel glorious and free. Sometimes it lasts only for an instant. As you slip off to sleep, a momentary ache leaves you wondering, "Will there ever be anything more to my life than projects I can't seem to complete, bills I can't seem to pay, and people I can't seem to please?" At other times, perhaps prompted by pain too deep for words, by failures too private to share, or simply by the soul-weariness of having more items on your to-do list than you can possibly accomplish in a single lifetime, the emptiness persists. That's when we find ourselves "in a wood so dark" for far longer than we expected. It's then that we wonder if, perhaps, when it comes to a life of glory, God has forgotten us.

Somewhere in a drawer I keep a photograph of two nine-year-old girls that I met at a landfill in Puerto Rico. Greicha is the one on the left; she's shorter, and her nose wrinkles as she giggles at the faces I'm making at her. Johanney is quieter; her shy smile barely shows behind Greicha's braids.

The coasts of Puerto Rico are the most beautiful I've ever seen—sandy beaches, white as new-fallen snow, heaving gently against unimaginably blue water. And yet, if I ever return to that picturesque island, it won't be the beaches or the water or the rain forests that I'll be looking for. No, what I will want to see most are the two children whose faces are framed in that photograph.

After several years of trying to run destitute people out of a landfill on the west side of town, the city of San Juan gave up. They covered the landfill with gravel and handed over ownership to hundreds of homeless families. These new landowners cobbled makeshift homes out of cast-off plywood and tin. The place still looked like a dump—but it was *their* dump now, and these landowners did their best to take care of it. And yet the living conditions remained unsanitary and unsafe. Our church didn't believe living in these conditions was acceptable, so we joined with several other congregations and headed to Puerto Rico to build new homes in the landfill neighborhoods.

Greicha and Johanney lived in a neighborhood beside the dump, and they spent most of the week working with me. Their desire to stick with me may have been influenced by the fact that I bought them ice cream and a native soda called Malta India at the end of each workday.

On my last day in the landfill, I took some pictures of Greicha and Johanney and told them that I would be flying home the next day. When the workday was nearly over, I asked the two girls what they wanted. I was thinking of ice cream bars and cold bottles of soda—but I was surprised.

"Don't forget us," Greicha said in her clipped English. "Keep us in your heart."

"Yes," Johanney chimed in. "Just don't forget us."

Introduction

Don't forget us.

"I won't," I said as I smiled—and I haven't. There's no way I could forget two little amber-skinned girls standing in a landfill, two children whose deepest desire wasn't anything I could purchase at a convenience store. It was simply that I keep them in my heart.

As I drove away in the van, windows down, I watched Greicha and Johanney waving their pop bottles and repeating, "Don't forget us! Don't forget!"

As the girls' voices faded, it occurred to me that perhaps this is the deepest cry of the human heart. *Don't forget me.* At various times in my life, I've etched my name on walls and carved my initials in the trunks of trees. I've recorded my life's events on weblogs and mercilessly pursued publishers with book proposals, longing to see my name etched on paper. And, if I'm perfectly honest with myself, what has compelled me in many of those moments is the same longing I heard from Greicha and Johanney.

Don't forget me.

We are—all of us—desperate not to be forgotten.

But I don't want to be remembered solely by other people. Most of all, I want to know that *God* remembers me. The moments when I feel the glory of life at its fullest are the moments when I am most aware that I'm remembered by a power far greater than any human being. But sometimes this glory, this awareness of God's presence, seems so distant. God feels so far off, the wood grows dark, and I find myself calling, "Please don't forget me," to a light that appears to be fading in the darkness.

That's where I found myself not too long ago.

I felt as if God, when deciding which prayers to answer and which lives to fill with glory, had forgotten about me.

Then, in the quiet beauty of ordinary life, something changed.

I saw no awe-inspiring visions, nor can I now claim to possess any secret key to the wisdom of the ages. But somewhere in the soul-weariness of these foolish attempts to find satisfaction I glimpsed this truth: The glory for which my soul was searching was hidden in the hullabaloo of the life I was already living.

God hadn't forgotten me. The entire time, his glory had waited in the chaos of life, longing for the moment when I would look beyond what my eyes could see. I had spent most of my life searching for something more glorious than my day-to-day life, only to discover it was precisely in the rhythms of my daily existence that the fullness of God's glory and life's splendor had always lingered.

This same glory is waiting in your life too.

You do not need one more series of steps to happiness, another rousing retreat, or the latest bestselling book to experience a life of glory. All you need is the life that you're already living and the Spirit who has already filled this life with more splendor than you ever imagined. All the glory for which your soul is searching is hidden in the hullabaloo of the life you're already living.

That's the glory of hullabaloo.

Are you ready to begin living in this glory?

If so, turn the page and let's begin!

Movement One

The Hunger for Glory

Once upon a time, I glimpsed your glory
from a mountaintop of my own making.
And it appeared to me that what I needed
to live a life of glory was
one more project,
one more possession,
one more accomplishment.
But these were detours that sent me
deep into the land of discontent.
More projects led to too much stress.
More possessions turned into too much stuff.
More accomplishments turned into too much of me.
Then I heard a simple voice,
still echoing in the distance:
"The glory you have given to me,
I have given to them"—
to me.
Swept up in the warm echo of that voice, I realized this:
One day, when I have learned to live as if
your glory always surrounds me,
I will move beyond
all of my stress,
all of my stuff,
all of myself.
And I will taste this truth:
Each moment that I spend in your shadow,
I am already living in your glory.

One

Emptiness: The Empty Field That Wasn't Empty After All

Glory is what we are after.

-Eugene Peterson, *Christ Plays in Ten Thousand Places*

My people have been lost sheep; ... they have forgotten their fold.... They have sinned against the Lord, the true pasture.

-Jeremiah, a Hebrew prophet

Jeremiah 50:6-7

I've found another couple I like better," the teenage girl's voice echoed in the telephone receiver, hollow and raw. "I want them to have my baby instead."

I groped for the words to respond.

There were none.

Somewhere between the telephone receiver and my ear, her words twisted into a jagged blade and ripped a ragged gash in my soul. All of my hopes and dreams flooded out of that wound.

Hopes for cradling an infant that my wife and I could call our own.

Dreams of filling the middle bedroom with pastel linens and tiny clothes.

Deep longings to fulfill God's command to rejoice in the raising of a child.

All of them surged upward and rushed down my face in the form of bitter tears.

A year earlier a doctor had informed us that we might not be able to have biological children. Despite the earnest efforts of physicians and the fervent prayers of family and friends, the pregnancy test never turned blue. Now, this teenager—this girl who had been blessed with a child she didn't even *want*—had shattered our dreams of adopting a child … again.

It wasn't the first time.

In the past six months two previous birth mothers had reneged on the same promise. In both cases they made their choices after the baby was born, once after we had named him and chosen his first clothes.

I stumbled across the living room and sank into the couch, telephone still clenched in my fist. Amid the decorative pillows and the laundry that would wait several weeks before being folded, I did not lose faith in God, but I did lose faith in life.

Although I still believed in God, I felt as though God had forgotten me.

For so long I had waited for something that I thought would satisfy my hunger for an ideal life—a baby we could call our own. Now, standing in the shadow of one more shattered dream, I no longer believed that life could be glorious or good. Perhaps *God* was glorious and good, but for reasons unknown to me, God had chosen to withhold any sense of glory from my life. "Be fruitful and multiply," God had charged humanity in the beginning (Gen. 1:28)—but now God had mocked our pain by crushing every prospect of obeying his own command.

I felt betrayed and abandoned by God, as if every hope of glory had been drained from my life. I don't recall everything I said to God in those moments, but I do suspect this: If Job had chosen to "curse God, and die" when he felt betrayed and abandoned by God (Job 2:9), the death he would have experienced would not have been the demise of his body or even the termination of his salvation. It would have been the death of his capacity to live in glory—to live in the persistent awareness of God's presence in every moment of life. At first, hurling angry accusations into the face of the Almighty is a carnal feast—a bacchanalian banquet for the darker side of your soul. The downside is that the carcass that remains at end of the feast tends to be that of your own innermost self, gutted of every semblance of glory.[1]

I sat in silence until Rayann returned home from work that night. She had stopped at Target to look at baby strollers. When she saw my face, the news was broken; we clung to each other, entwined in a living knot of sorrow. What we made that night was not quite love, but it had once lived in the same neighborhood as love. As such, it stilled—if only for a moment—the horrible, haunting emptiness that had sapped our spirits and raped our souls.

Starving for Glory

My position as pastor of a rapidly growing church provided our primary income during those months. Despite the precarious position of my own faith, there were classes to be taught, programs to be planned, and Bible studies to be prepared. So I continued to study the Scriptures. I had to; studying Scripture was in my job description, after all. Perhaps believing that life could be filled with divine glory should have been in my job description, but it wasn't. It was most likely for the best since I no longer believed in such fantasies anyway.

Oddly enough, my refusal to believe that life could be glorious didn't keep me from looking for glory and goodness in life. When I say *glory,* I don't mean *celebrity* or *popularity*; those are what previous generations called "vain glory."[2] They are cheap mockeries of an authentic awareness of God's availability in every moment of our lives. Such supposed experiences of "glory" represent the "sweet poison of the false infinite"[3]—the soul-slaying delusion that there is real significance to be found in the fleeting trinkets of human status and celebrity. What I mean by glory in this context isn't even the momentary glimpses of God's presence that have caused saints to worship and sinners to quake—though those experiences of divine splendor have sometimes prompted the sense that I'm describing here.

What I mean by glory is a deep inner awareness of the closeness of a presence greater than myself. It's what Moses craved when he whispered in the shadow of Mount Sinai, "Show me your glory" (Ex. 33:18). "God, I know that you are fully present in every moment," Moses seems to have been saying. "Now, let me see this presence." And I still longed for that awareness of God's availability in every moment of my life. I deeply desired that sense, in the words of C. S. Lewis, of "approval or (I might say) appreciation by God."[4] I longed to know that God had not forgotten me.

This longing is not (I realized later) unique to my soul. One religious scholar has written,

> There is within us—in even the blithest, most lighthearted among us—a fundamental dis-ease. This desire lies in the marrow of our bones and deep in the regions of our soul. We are seldom in direct touch with it, and indeed the modern world seems set on preventing us from getting in touch with it by covering it with … entertainments, obsessions, and distractions of every sort. But the longing is there, built into us like a jack-in-the-box that presses for release.[5]

Despite my lack of faith in the possibility of God's goodness, I could not escape this longing for glory.

Neither can you.

God, Our Grazing Land

Whenever God and I aren't on speaking terms, I typically end up plowing through the writings of an ancient Hebrew prophet named Jeremiah. I've found in him a soul mate of sorts. Jeremiah spends most of his ministry meandering back and forth across the borderland between intense passion and overwhelming despair. Before he even reaches adulthood, God has called him to prophesy the destruction of his own people. You'd think that a man with this sort of mission would become jaded, numbed to the pain around him. Yet Jeremiah never finds it in himself to respond to life's pains with pious platitudes or spiritual clichés. He argues with God, despises God's message, and adores God's glory, all while wrestling with his pain in passion and rage—sometimes in the same chapter. It's as if Jeremiah is intent—in the words of Bruce Cockburn and Bono—on "kicking the darkness 'til it bleeds daylight."[6] He is constantly torn between his longing never to prepare another sermon and the burning of a divine message deep within in his bones (Jer. 20:9). "Why, why this chronic pain, this ever worsening wound and no healing in sight?" he weeps. "You're nothing, GOD, but a mirage, a lovely oasis in the distance—and then nothing!" (Jer. 15:18 MSG).

There are times when I'm pretty certain I know how he felt.

It was during one of my many readings of Jeremiah's prophecies that I stumbled across this phrase: "The Lord, the true pasture" (Jer. 50:7), or "The Lord, their righteous grazing land," according to the *Holman Christian Standard Bible*.[7]

I puzzled for several days over this phrase. Here was a metaphor for God that I'd never considered before. God as a king, a rock, a shield—those similes I understood.

But God as a pasture?

A grazing land?

A *field*?

The Lord of glory, a tract of grassland?

The living God, spattered with the dung of sheep and goats?

"The Lord, the true pasture"?

I didn't know what to do with this image.

One morning, a week or so after I first noticed this phrase, I slipped out of the house before dawn and made my way to a nearby park. "God is my field," I murmured as my eyes swept a vast carpet of grass, recently mown and unmoving. It was early autumn. The leaves still fluttered from the branches of sleek Bradford pear trees and stately maples, tinges of yellow and orange barely beginning to creep along their delicate tips. I breathed deeply, drawing the tingling fragrances of grass and earth into my innermost being.

Why, of all things, a field?

I fell to my knees amid the scattered clippings of Bermuda grass and stared at the earth beneath me. Here, as the morning sun began to lift its gaze upon the field, I felt anger at God's failure to answer my prayers uncoil within me again, writhing in my soul like a livid serpent.

"Yes, God, you are a field," I hissed. "No matter how many times I come to you, no matter how badly I hurt, no matter how hard I look for you, you lie there, silent, unmoving—just like a field. You do *nothing!* I cannot deny you; I wish I could. But, oh, how I hate you. I … *hate* … you!"

And I spat on the ground.

I stared at the spot where my spit hit the ground, and I noticed an insect, translucent and so small that it was barely visible to human eyes. As I traced the contours of this tiny bug, I began to see other creatures amid the grass clippings, minute creatures pursuing their various vocations beneath the visible surface, unheralded and unnoted.

Despite all appearances to the contrary, the very earth around me teemed with activity, with beauty, with *life*.

As I gazed into this scrap of ground, a voice seemed to rise from the earth itself. Not an audible voice—no, it was a voice deeper and more powerful than any my ear had ever perceived. It was at once utterly silent and undeniably real.

"Yes, I am like a field," the silent voice seemed to say. "Even when it seems as if I am doing nothing, even when you feel like I am ignoring you, even when you curse my name, I am full of life. I am working beneath the surface of your life in ways that you may never see. Yes, my child, I *am* like a field."

In this moment I drew my chin to my chest, and the ground where I knelt became holy ground. I was still uncertain about God's goodness, and I still saw scant evidence of divine glory in my daily life. But I wanted to live in divine glory, and I believed that somehow, someday, I might.

For now, that was enough.

The Lingering Longing

Five months after I knelt in that newly mown field an unexpected prospect emerged. A family in another state had adopted a Romanian orphan and then abandoned her. Would we be interested in an older child? Mounds of paperwork alternated between manic preparations, and just a few weeks later, a spunky seven-year-old girl named Hannah lugged a hand-me-down suitcase from who-knows-where up the front steps of our house.

Hannah had some difficulties, no doubt about it. Then again, after the pains of the past couple of years, so did I, which is possibly why we so quickly made quite the pair. If the law would have allowed it, I would have adopted her after the first weekend she stayed with us, but the social worker said we had to wait six months.

I grew pretty fond of that kid during those months, to tell you the truth. Some people even said that I spoiled her, but I didn't, of course. I just made up for all the hugs and kisses and snuggles and Christmases and birthdays and other special days that others had skipped during Hannah's first seven years. Or maybe what I was trying to make up for were my own heart's longings, which were so brutally mangled each time a birth mother had changed her mind. Either way, I delighted in this child's love, and I'm quite certain that she delighted in mine.

And yet a deep emptiness lingered in the depths of my soul.

Somehow I imagined that what my soul craved was a child to call my own. Now, this child was mine, but something was still missing. I prayed, I studied the Scriptures, and I read books on spiritual formation. I searched more books than I care to recall, looking for some series of steps that would satisfy my soul, but the discontent lingered.

I was still hungry for something more.

What I still craved was *glory*—the persistent awareness of God's availability in every moment of my life.

But what else did I need?

If I could not find the glory of life in this child whom I loved so much, where could I find it?

The answer was nearer than I had ever imagined.

All the Colors

Six months after Hannah moved into our house, we found ourselves standing in the chambers of a county judge declaring ourselves to be the parents of this child. On the way home that evening we watched the setting sun spin a fiery kaleidoscope of colors across the western sky.

"God sure made a pretty sky tonight, didn't he?" I said.

"Mm-hmm," a sleepy voice murmured from the backseat. Hannah curled up against her pink Kim Possible pillow, and there was a long silence. Suddenly, Hannah sat up.

"Daddy, know what? God put red in the sky tonight—that's Mommy's favorite color. There's blue for you. Over there is pink; that's for me."

"Everyone's favorite colors are in the sky tonight, aren't they?"

"Uh-huh. Know what else, Daddy? I think God's happy tonight because all the colors are finally together. How 'bout you?" Several moments passed before a reply wedged its way past the lump in my throat.

"Yes, Hannah, I'm happy too," I said. "I'm happy too."

"So, will you always be my daddy now?"

"Yes, for always. For always."

As this child slipped into the contentment of sleep, something happened within my soul. I cannot explain what happened; I cannot reduce it to a series of steps or a marketable paradigm for spiritual healing. But there—somewhere between the innocent observation of my daughter and the luminous wonder of a southwestern sunset—I finally tasted the truth about how God had been working in my life. I realized that Hannah hadn't become my daughter on this day in the chambers of a county judge. No, Hannah was my girl from the moment she was conceived in some unknown village on the other side of the world; I simply didn't know it yet. During all those months of screaming into what seemed like silence, God had already answered my prayers with this child. God was not silent because he had chosen not to speak; God seemed silent because he had already spoken. All that time, he had been working silently, unseen, beneath the surface, like the life that teems in a field beneath each blade of grass.

Somehow, in this, I also glimpsed a far deeper truth—the truth about the glory my soul had craved so deeply. *This glory was available here and now, in this moment—and it always had been, not only in this moment but also in every moment before this one.*

I thought about the many things I had, at different times, thought I needed to satisfy the deepest longings of my soul—a spouse, a house, one more degree, one more dollar, a specific job, a child to parent. As I considered these gifts, I was forced to make a painful admission: Some of these gifts had served, for a few weeks, months, or even years, to divert my attention from my deepest inner longings. Others had provided fleeting glimpses into a life of glory, but none of these gifts had truly satisfied my soul.

Somewhere in the depths of my being I had known this all along. But this time there was something more, something I hadn't seen until now: *The glory for which my soul had been searching had always been hidden in the life that I was already living.* All these years the glory of life had been waiting in my present life, longing for the moment when I would look beyond what my eyes could see. Everything I needed to satisfy my soul I already possessed. But I never noticed it because I always thought I needed something more. I had expected this child to bring glory into my life, but she hadn't. Why? Because the glory for which I was searching was already present in the life I was living—I simply hadn't been willing to see it.

In the ruddy splendor of that setting sun a new awareness of the full wonder of life began to dawn. And, ever so slowly, an awareness of divine glory began to seep into the parched recesses of my soul. I cannot claim that I have always lived in divine glory from that moment forward. Despite my moments of progress, I am still struggling to live every moment of life swept up in divine glory. I have not yet arrived at my goal of living "ordinary life in a supernatural way"—but I do know where this glory is found.[8] I have tasted this truth: *As long as Jesus Christ lives in me, all that I need to live a life of glory—all that I need to live each present moment in the infinite satisfaction of God's presence—is already available in the life that I'm presently living*. This recognition set me on a quest for glory that continues today. This book is my attempt to share one portion of this quest with you.

Be forewarned, though: The quest for a glorious life does not follow a smooth and orderly path. This journey leads not only beside placid waters but also through valleys of darkness and death. As in the most magnificent of sunsets, God often whirls together hues and shades on this pathway that no interior decorator would dream of approving. Somehow the festive colors we had planned don't quite make it onto the Master Artist's palette, and in the midst of our darkness, his shadowed hues can seem dubious at best.

But one day in the stillness of your soul, perhaps you will see it too—a design, as clear and colossal as the wildest and most wonderful of sunsets. In that moment you will glimpse the truth—the very combinations you questioned and even cursed were part of an answer that God was forming long before you even knew the words to make your request.

And the results?

They're nothing less than glorious.

This doesn't make the quest any more predictable, but it does make the moments of darkness a little bit easier to swallow.

Two

Glory: When Your Messiah Drives a Minivan

GOD CROWDS UPON US FROM SHEOL TO THE SEA.... HE VEILS HIMSELF IN FLESH, THE SAME FLESH THAT DRIPS INTO FINGERS AT THE END OF MY ARMS AND SPROUTS INTO HAIR ON MY HEAD.

-VIRGINIA STEM OWENS, *And the Trees Clap Their Hands*

GOD ... IS NOT FAR FROM EACH ONE OF US. FOR "IN HIM WE LIVE AND MOVE AND HAVE OUR BEING."

-THE APOSTLE PAUL

Acts 17:27-28

Heat shimmers upward from the pavement, birthing miniature mirages that dance madly between bumpers and fenders in an endless chain of automobiles. A revolving bank sign reveals that the time is 4:12 p.m., alternately flashing a temperature of 105 degrees. If my child registered a temperature of this magnitude, I would rush her to the emergency room, bathing her brow with a cool cloth. But this is Oklahoma on a late-summer afternoon, and such temperatures are mere footnotes on the five o'clock news.

The conflicting messages on the bumper stickers and the varying rhythms of the heads bobbing above the drivers' seats divulge the diversity of this area. Hummers and Harleys wait alongside mud-spattered pickup trucks and compact cars long past their prime.

Nothing here seems glorious. It is an ordinary afternoon filled with ordinary people trying to find their way home amid the hubbub and hullabaloo of their ordinary lives.

My seven-year-old sits beside me in the car, face upturned as she sings along with the latest single by U2. As our car curves to the right, something on the opposite side of the intersection seizes Hannah's attention.

"Look!" she points toward a battered minivan, a fading remnant of that brief moment in the 1980s when Americans inexplicably used the words *minivan* and *cool* in the same sentence. "Look! There's *Jesus*."

I glimpse just enough of the vehicle's lone occupant to grasp the reason for her momentary delusion. The driver is long-haired, bearded, and olive-skinned, white teeth glinting through a gentle smile.

The Jesus of a thousand Sunday school take-home papers.

Without thinking, I smile and reply, "No, Hannah. That

wasn't Jesus. It *can't* be. Jesus lived on the earth a long time ago … almost two thousand years ago. It was just someone who looks like the *paintings* of Jesus."

"But," Hannah is staring through the rear window, eyes still riveted to the minivan, "it *was* Jesus! I saw him."

"No, Hannah," my tone is harsher than I intend. "It wasn't Jesus. It couldn't have been."

The minivan vanishes into the jumble of vehicles crisscrossing the intersection, and Hannah coils back into her seat with a whisper, "But, Daddy, it *was.*" As her moment of childlike wonder chokes in a sea of grown-up logic, a gentle murmur wends its way past the dry bones of a soul that once found magic wands in the branches of ordinary trees and glorious wonders amid the stars of a common sky.

What if she's right?

What if God's presence is nearer than I ever imagined?

Years of rational thinking and theological training recoil at this thought, this alien intruder from a childhood long past. *God in a minivan! That's as absurd as … as …* The other voice—the voice of childlike wonder—whispers again, *As absurd as the glory of God erupting from a flaming shrub on the far side of a Middle Eastern desert? As absurd as the Messiah, enfolded in the flesh of a peasant's baby, tumbling into a feed trough in Bethlehem? As insane as the King of the Universe screaming from a wooden stake, stabbed like a dagger into the heart of the Hill of the Skull? As crazy as all the other wonders that you claim to believe, that you've embalmed in the pages of your theology but that you're unwilling to look for here and now?*

"But then again, Hannah," I hear a voice speaking and realize that it must be my own, "who knows? Maybe it was." And suddenly an ordinary afternoon is filled with extraordinary possibilities. For I find myself realizing anew—even, in some shadowed corner of my soul, *believing*—that God is always present, always available, even in the moments when I least expect it.

What I am experiencing is a reminder of *glory.*

Created for Glory

I suspect that, at some point, you've also felt this way. You have experienced a moment in which you found yourself suspecting that God's presence was nearer than you had ever imagined. You were reminded of glory.

What I'm describing as *glory* is the awareness that God is fully present and available in every present moment of life. It's the feeling of smallness that overwhelms me as I stand on the ocean shore, the sand and surf kneading my weary feet, causing me to feel as though I can almost trace the very face of God. It's the catch that swells in my throat as I nestle my nose into my wife's cascade of hair and recall that this woman is a gift from God—a gift far more wonderful than anything I have ever deserved. It's the realization that the history behind us and the world around us are too wonderful and wild to be explained by logic alone. It's the momentary recognition that, if I worship a God who's been known to reveal his glory in common shrubs, cattle troughs, and Galilean carpenters, there's really no place so lowly or earthbound that he can't show up.[1] It's the inner recognition that a divine presence is nearer than I ever imagined and that there is no presence in heaven or on earth that matters more.[2]

You *have* tasted glory, haven't you?

There is, however, a greater truth implied in these encounters—a truth that you may not have realized yet.

What is this truth?

You remember these experiences because you were created for glory.

You don't believe it?

Neither do I sometimes, but let's try anyway.

Whisper this truth to yourself until some segment of your soul believes it: *I was created for glory.*

Are you still struggling to accept this truth? If so, take a look at some comments from your Creator: According to the hymn of an ancient Hebrew king, glory is a crown that God has placed on the head of every human being (Ps. 8:5).

Once, when God's people began to doubt his love for them, he whispered these words into his prophet's ear: "I will bring your offspring from the east, and from the west I will gather you.... Everyone who is called by my name, whom I created *for my glory*" (Isa. 43:5, 7). It was glory that shone from the face of Moses on Sinai and glory that one of Jesus' first followers longed to enshrine on the Mount of Transfiguration (Ex. 33—34; Luke 9:30–33).

One of God's motives in bringing people to himself was—according to Peter and Paul, two pillars among the early followers of Jesus—precisely so that humanity could experience glory (1 Thess. 2:12; 2 Thess. 2:14; 1 Peter 5:10). And it isn't only believers in God that experience divine splendor; pagans glimpse God's glory too. The only difference is that the nonbeliever misconstrues its true source (Rom. 1:20–23). That's what the apostle Paul meant when he said that, even though God's "invisible attributes ... have been clearly perceived," humanity has "exchanged the glory of the immortal God for images" (Rom. 1:20, 23 ESV). Later, Paul even claimed that the essence of sin is to fall short of the glory for which God created us (Rom. 3:23).

You long for glory because you were formed for glory.

You were created for glory.

What's more, you weren't created to only experience glory in the ephemeral glimmers that pierce your ordinary existence for a brief moment. You weren't even created to postpone your experiences of glory until some point in the future—perhaps on the far side of your funeral service or sometime after Jesus' return. You were created to live every moment in glory, here and now.

You, with all the haunting failures that bind you to your past by casting dark shadows across your present ... *you* were created to live in glory. You, with all of your doubts about yourself and—in those moments you would rather not admit—about your God ... *you* were created to live in glory. You, who sleep with your harshest critic on the nights when you sleep alone ... *you* were created to live every moment of your life in glory. "Christians," Eugene Peterson mused, "don't have to wait until after [their] funerals to get in on the glory. As St. Teresa, one of our most irreverent and audacious saints, used to say, 'The pay starts in this life.'"[3]

And what *is* the "pay" that starts in this life? What happens when you embrace the full availability of God in every present moment? What is the result of learning to live in glory? The payoff is peace, harmony, contentment—satisfaction of all the soul cravings that seem so unattainable amid the hullabaloo of your daily life.

The Glory around You

You were created to live every moment in glory, here and now.

I know, I know—it sounds crazy to me, too. And I already

hear your voice of protest: "Live every moment in glory? That sounds great! But *how*? Right now, I'm barely surviving each moment of my life, and you're expecting me to live each moment in glory? How can I possibly move beyond the projects I can't seem to complete, the bills I can't seem to pay, and the people I can't seem to please?"

My answer?

You don't have to.

You don't have to move beyond the constant stream of unpleasant people, unfinished projects, and outstanding bills flooding your daily life. You don't have to move beyond the doubts, the waiting, and the unwelcome interruptions that seem to reduce every remnant of glory to rubble. You don't have to move beyond anything because the glory for which your soul was created is already present around you, filling every moment of your life with unimaginable wonder. It took several years for me to come to terms with this truth, but I have never been more certain than I am right now that it is, in fact, the truth.

Wasn't that Paul's point when he proclaimed to the philosophers of Athens, "In [God] we live and move and have our being" (Acts 17:28)? If it truly is in *God* that I live and move and exist, there is no portion of my life where divine glory does not swirl in and around me. God "dwells within the seed of the smallest flower and is not cramped," a character in one of C. S. Lewis's novels claims. "Deep Heaven is inside Him who is inside the seed and does not distend Him."[4]

Do you recognize what this means for my day-to-day life?

Infinite glory is present and available within every moment of my life.

That momentary flash on the horizon that just caught my attention? My mind tells me to ascribe it to a stray meteor, aging corneas, perhaps a peculiar reflection on my windshield. Yet what if, just for a moment, the three dimensions in which I live couldn't contain God's splendor? What if, in that instant, the point of demarcation between the visible world and eternity suddenly ruptured? What if, in that fleeting glimmer, I glimpsed glory?

And the odd whistling that I hear amid the pecan trees? My brain tells me that it's nothing more than some curious combination of the breeze and rustling leaves. But what if these trees are filled with myriads of six-winged seraphim, dancing upon unseen blazes of divine majesty? What if this nut-strewn orchard in which I feel so alone is actually alive, seething with the presence of God?

If it truly is "in him" that I live and move and exist, every quark and atom in the universe is a theater of God's glory.[5] Every particle of this planet—even the air that I breathe—is stretched to the point of bursting with the possibility of God's presence. It is as if the cosmos is a vast womb on the verge of erupting with divine splendor. All creation is, in the words of the apostle Paul, "groaning in labor pains," longing for the revelation of God's glory (Rom. 8:22).

Above you there is glory. "The heavens are telling the glory of God" (Ps. 19:1). Around you there is glory embedded in the daily rhythms of eating and drinking, resting and working (1 Cor. 10:31). If you have joined your life with the life of Jesus, there is glory within you. Even now, the Spirit of God is molding a reflection of God in you (2 Cor. 3:18).

Every morning, there is glory in your house. Your child's hand is splayed like a starfish upon her pillow as she sleeps, her chest rising and falling in a gentle rhythm of rest. You step into her room to wake her, and you are faced with a choice: You can shake her into groggy wakefulness and begin your morning ritual of screaming at the children, kicking the dog, and rushing out the door with breakfast clenched between your teeth. You can teach your family the great American lie that what really matters in life is hurrying through today's list of tasks so they can rush through an even longer list tomorrow. If you train your child in this way of life, she can enjoy the dubious privilege of living and dying with a calendar that is full and a soul that is empty. She becomes one more captive of the deadly delusion that what makes her valuable is how much she accomplishes.

How can you embrace the glory that surrounds you in such a moment?

You can remember that this apparently ordinary morning is actually a moment of glory, a moment that can never be repeated, an instant in which all the wonder of creation is available for you to embrace.

As you look at your child, you can choose to stand in awe of how God has slipped the unimaginably glorious gift of this child into your life; you can ask yourself how the tiny bundle of flesh grew up so quickly; you can bury your face in the hair that still smells of strawberry shampoo and whisper a blessing upon her day.

You can choose to see glory.

In the past, God has revealed his glory not only in raging storms and burning bushes but also through stubborn donkeys (Ex. 3:1–4; Num. 22:23–28; Job 38:1; 1 Kings 19:12).

And today?

God embeds his glory "in cooking and small talk, through storytelling, making love, fishing, tending animals and sweet corn and flowers, through sports, music and books, raising kids—all the places where the gravy soaks in and grace shines through,"[6] to borrow Garrison Keillor's picturesque description. There is glory in your home and glory in your job, glory in the earth and glory in the people around you.

Virginia Stem Owens comments,

> [God] hides in the bushes, jumping out in flames to startle us into seeing. He sequesters himself in stables and swaddling so as to take us unawares. He veils himself in flesh, the same flesh that drips into fingers at the end of my arms and sprouts into hair on my head.[7]

Who knows?

Such a God might even use the ordinary moments in your life and mine to reveal his glory. He might even use a child's overactive imagination as she glimpses a bearded stranger in a minivan. There is, after all, glory all around us, all the time, filling every molecule and every moment of life with infinite splendor.

Three

Hullabaloo: Learning the Art of Life

All happenings, great and small, are parables whereby God speaks. The art of life is to get the message.

—Malcolm Muggeridge
"News Summaries"

This slight momentary affliction is preparing us for an eternal weight of glory beyond all measure.

—Apostle Paul
2 Corinthians 4:17

Infinite glory is available to us in every moment—that much seems clear. But there's a difficulty with this line of thinking: If divine glory is so accessible, why do we so rarely glimpse this glory? And, even when we do glimpse the glory around us, why do these glimpses seem to have so little effect on our lives? Why do we return so quickly to the soul-sapping rhythms of constant busyness and stress?

The problem, it seems, is *hullabaloo.*

Hullabaloo—no one knows for certain where the word comes from. It seems to have descended from the eighteenth-century Scottish phrase "hollo ballo"—a term that could depict exuberance, chaos, or simply the daily hubbub of an overly busy life.[1] In these pages, I'm using the word to portray the ordinary stuff of life, the portions of your life that you may not think about until they occur, the daily rhythms that consume the larger portion of your time.

Hullabaloo is the time you spend drumming your thumbs on the steering wheel as you wait for the light to change, rushing to the doctor's office to mend a wounded finger, rousing your spouse in the morning to rehearse today's to-do list before realizing that no single day can possibly provide enough hours to accomplish all the tasks. It's the struggling, the doubting, the waiting, and the interruptions that press through the surface of life like weeds in a fallow field. It's the stuff that slips into life between the birthdays and graduations and family reunions. It's the seconds time will slowly meld into elusive impressions lurking in the murkier regions of your memory. The hullabaloo isn't always evil, and it isn't always good. It's simply a reminder that life is always moving. And it's hullabaloo that seems to crowd out our awareness of divine glory.

Most of the time we don't think much about these

moments of discomfort and doubt, impatience and interruptions. When the winds of hullabaloo press against us, we complain. The rest of the time we simply endure the hullabaloo as we make our way from one facet of life to another, always searching for something more glorious than the rhythms of ordinary life.

And that is precisely the problem.

Why?

Because the glory of life is hidden within the hullabaloo.

All the glory for which our souls are searching is present and available within the hullabaloo of the lives we are already living.

And this glory—this gift of God's own self, hidden in the depths of the ordinary events of our lives—has the capacity to fill our souls with the contentment and peace we so deeply crave.

It's as if we've trained ourselves simply to tolerate the ordinary rhythms of our lives as we wait for something greater, something better, something more. Yet the hullabaloo in your life was never meant merely to be endured. And, though you may occasionally reduce a bit of your life's hullabaloo, the hullabaloo wasn't meant to be escaped either. The hullabaloo—each part of your day that seems so random and ordinary, so meaningless and mundane—has been filled with God's presence for the purpose of reminding you that you live every moment of your life "in him."

Glory is not something that may happen someday, beyond this present existence. Glory is present wherever God is present, and God has hidden his presence in the hullabaloo of your life. The only reason it's difficult to notice God's glory amid the hullabaloo is the same reason a fish would most likely be the last creature to discover water. Not because it is in short supply around you, but because you live every moment of your life in it.

The glory of life hides within the hullabaloo.

In *The Voyage of the Dawn Treader* in C. S. Lewis's series *The Chronicles of Narnia,* the children encounter a retired star named Ramandu. When Ramandu tells them that he was once a star, one child exclaims, "In our world, … a star is a huge ball of flaming gas." To this Ramandu replies, "Even in your world, my son, that is not what a star *is* but what a star is *made of*."[2] The same might be said about the relationship between glory and hullabaloo in your life. Hullabaloo may be what your life is *made of,* but glory describes the essence of what your life *is*. And what is available amid the hullabaloo is none other than God himself.

What God Sees When He Looks at the World

There's a difference between how God looks at our circumstances and how we look at the same circumstances: Where we see only an endless stream of struggles and doubts, needless waiting and interruptions, God sees lives filled with glory. If you don't believe this is God's view of the world, take a look at God's track record: When the serpent's soft-whispered lie shattered the serenity of Eden, God surveyed the mess Adam and Eve had made of his creation and saw the possibility of humanity's salvation (Gen. 3:1–15). God looked at Sarah—a postmenopausal woman with doubts about God's fertility program and a tendency to laugh at all the wrong times—and saw the mother of a mighty nation (Gen. 18:10–15). He ran across a shepherd boy waiting in the fields of Bethlehem and looked past a harp and sling to see a man who would be king (1 Sam. 16:10–13).

God saw the glory in the hullabaloo.

When God planted his feet on earth in the flesh of

Jesus of Nazareth, his penchant for glimpsing glory in the hullabaloo didn't show any signs of slowing. In fact, in Jesus Christ, God demonstrated even more clearly how he persistently pours the power of his presence out among ordinary lives (see Luke 17:19–21). Once, Jesus glanced at a cluster of ordinary lilies and saw signs of his Father's providence (Matt. 6:28–30). Another time, when a sound like distant thunder interrupted his teaching, Jesus sensed the very voice of God, proclaiming his glory through the groaning of the cosmos (John 12:27–29). Most amazing of all, Jesus looked toward the moment of his suffering and identified it as a moment of glory (John 12:23).

And today?

God looks at the likes of you and me and glimpses boundless possibilities for his glory in precisely the places where we see only the hullabaloo of our ordinary lives. In the words of the apostle Paul, "this slight momentary affliction" (that's Paul's way of saying "hullabaloo") "is preparing for us an eternal weight of glory beyond all measure" (2 Cor. 4:17).

May I paraphrase Paul's point? *It's the hullabaloo around us that can cultivate the glory within us.* There is glory in the hullabaloo.

I think, perhaps, that's what the genealogies in the Gospels are trying to tell us too (see Matt. 1:1–16; Luke 3:23–38). (Yes, the *genealogies*—those interminable lists of names where your New Year's resolution to read through the entire Bible in one year typically meets an untimely demise.) The genealogies cover not only the years of Israel's military triumphs and covenant faithfulness, but also a good bit of hullabaloo—centuries of ordinary living and dying interspersed with times when God seemed utterly silent. However, when viewed in light of the arrival of Jesus, these genealogies remind us that even in the moments when God seems silent, glory waits beneath the surface of life. Through "Achim who begat Eliud who begat Eleazar" and all the other *begats* and *begans* that bog down even the most dogged Bible readers, God was forming the household and the nation where a divine Messiah would, for the most infinitesimal speck of time, find his home. And once God showed up on planet Earth, those who were willing to look beyond the face of an ordinary carpenter glimpsed nothing less than glory. They saw the presence of God amid the hullabaloo of their ordinary lives (John 1:14).

Getting the Message

When I say there is glory available amid the ordinary hubbub and hullabaloo of your life, I'm not promoting the notion that every happening in your life is good. The God who revealed his character in Jesus of Nazareth never promised that every event in your life would—or even should—be good. (This is, after all, the same deity whose own path led him to a borrowed tomb by means of a Roman execution stake.)

What I *am* claiming is that glory is not some fleeting experience that floats beyond your grasp for the briefest moment before fading into the hullabaloo. Even in life's most unpredictable moments, infinite glory is present and available like a sparkling stream that pulses constantly beneath the surface of our daily lives. Sin has twisted our world until not only our individual souls, but also states and nations and nature are tainted by darkness. Yet not even this pervasive darkness can completely eclipse the fact that God's creation is rich in glory and "very good" (Gen. 1:31). Because God's creation is glorious and good, our lives on this planet are glorious gifts—gifts that God intends to be free from worry, free from fear, and free to see the glory around us (see Matt. 6:24–34).

What I'm calling for in these pages is a renewed approach to the Christian life—one that recognizes the truth that, if the Spirit of God lives in you, everything you need to live the life God intends for you is already available in your present life. You don't need another conference, another curriculum, or another spiritual discipline. You don't even need this book. All you need is the life you're already living and the God who has already filled your life with more glory than you could ever imagine. God has given me the gift of life, and if I am a follower of Jesus, he's given me the gift of himself. To live a life of glory I need nothing else.

The more I take this truth seriously, the more I recognize how many moments of life I have wasted because I did not believe there was anything glorious to be found here and now. I have set my heart on locating the ideal job, earning the highest degrees, purchasing the perfect house, and building the best possible family. In the process I've missed the fleeting instances of divine glory that remained unseen because the only splendor I could envision was the empty pleasure of accomplishing my own plans. I missed the glory in the hullabaloo.

"All happenings, great and small, are parables by which God speaks," theologian Malcolm Muggeridge once stated. "The art of life is to get the message."[3] We need to begin to get the message hidden in the hullabaloo. That means sensing the groaning of the cosmos in the day-to-day rhythms of our lives and living as if, somewhere beneath these longings, something greater waits. It means learning to look at our struggles and our doubts, our impatience and our interruptions with eyes that trace the hidden strands of glory in each event. It's learning to live as if the hullabaloo is filled with glory … because, after all, it is.

Isn't that the point of Jesus' parables about his kingdom? Jesus never described his glorious kingdom in terms of tidy logical sequences or quick secrets to successful living. Instead, he told stories drawn from the hullabaloo of ordinary life. According to Jesus, his kingdom is like a mustard seed sprouting beside a busy road, like a lump of yeast spreading throughout a batch of dough, like a treasure that waits beneath the soil for the one person who is willing to let go of everything to possess it (Matt. 13:31–33, 44). All of these illustrations involve ordinary objects that aren't easily managed or marketed. Yet in each one the glory of God's kingdom is hidden. And if God's glory is available in a tiny seed, a lump of leaven, or a box buried in a field, is it really too much of a stretch to believe that his glory is present in your life and mine?

The person who truly experiences divine glory is, as Leonard Sweet writes, "someone who is awake to the voice that everyone hears. Someone who looks for the dance of glory in precisely the places where everyone else hears only the redundant rhythms of another day."[4]

An English journalist named G. K. Chesterton made much the same point: "It is a strange thing that many truly spiritual men … have actually spent some hours in speculating upon the precise location of the garden of Eden. Most probably we are in Eden still. It is only our eyes that have changed."[5] As I consider the implications of the glory in the hullabaloo, I think that perhaps Chesterton was right. I have spent so many years staring at the smudges on the window glass of my life, focusing on the imperfections in myself and in the people around me. In the process I have failed to look *through* the glass where infinite splendor has been awaiting the moment when my eyes become willing to see.

Four

More: Why Nothing at the Convenience Store Can Satisfy Your Hunger

OH, LORD, YOU HAVE MADE US FOR YOURSELF, AND OUR HEARTS ARE RESTLESS UNTIL THEY FIND THEIR REST IN YOU.

-AUGUSTINE OF HIPPO

YOU'LL WORSHIP ALL KINDS OF OTHER GODS, GODS NEITHER YOU NOR YOUR PARENTS EVER HEARD OF, WOOD AND STONE NO-GODS. BUT ... YOU'LL NOT BE ABLE TO SETTLE DOWN. GOD WILL GIVE YOU A RESTLESS HEART, LONGING EYES, A HOMESICK SOUL.

-MOSES

DEUTERONOMY 28:64-65 MSG

The morning sun rolled a blanket of gold across northern New Mexico. Indigo peaks shifted to fiery crimson, and for the first time I understood the phrase "purple mountain majesties." The landscape before me looked as if the Master Artist was hurling hues across the horizon with all the zest of a two-year-old who has just discovered the joys of finger painting.

I staggered down the steps of the church van. The day before, a dozen eager youth and half a dozen haggard sponsors had seen the rolling hills of eastern Oklahoma fade into the scrubby wastelands of northern Texas. Arizona was today's destination. There, we planned to spend the next week or so roofing and renovating houses for low-income homeowners in Phoenix.

I arched my aching back and opened my mouth wide, inviting the morning air to cleanse my nostrils and lungs. Tulsa was less than ten hours behind us, and the van's interior already reeked like a locker-room floor.

That's when I saw him.

A Native American, perhaps forty years old, filthy blanket draped across his coat, shabby fedora resting sideways on a wild mane of salt-and-pepper hair.

He was stumbling toward the girls' van when I stepped into his path. A childlike smile spread across the man's face, unveiling a forlorn trio of yellow teeth.

"Eighteen cents," he grunted before I could ask him what he needed.

I almost pulled a quarter from my pocket. Then, I hesitated. Amid the swirling stenches of vomit and stale urine, I caught the sickeningly sweet fragrance of cheap wine.

"What for?" I asked. He uncoiled a quivering fist and stared at a mound of pennies, nickels, and dimes.

"Got dollar and eight-two cents. Need eighteen cents more."

I repeated my query, "What for?"

"Hangover from last night, hurting me," he slurred. "Need two dollars for a bottle of wine. Make me feel better."

I wanted to turn away from the man's deep-creviced face. I wanted to seize his shoulders and shake some sense into this shattered descendant of the noble people that once wandered these mountain ranges. I wanted to throw up in disgust—not at the man himself but at what his addiction had reduced him to.

I did admire his honesty, though.

"Come with me to that store," I suggested as I nodded toward a nearby gas station. "I'll buy you anything you want to eat or drink, as long as it's not going to get you drunk again."

He chuckled nervously, "No, just need eighteen cents. Really need a drink."

"Let me get you something better," I pleaded. "Doughnuts, sandwiches, chips, pop—whatever you want, as much as you want."

The man shook his head, backed away from me, and lurched haphazardly across the parking lot.

And me?

I pressed my shoulder against a light-pole where a faded poster from a concert long past flapped in the breeze, and I choked. This man—this creature so lovingly crafted in the image of God—thought he needed a few more cents for one more drink to numb his pain.

In truth, he *was* hungry … but not for any food that I could have found at the convenience store.

Believe it or not, so are you.

You are hungry.

Famished.

Starving, in fact. But, please, at least finish this chapter before you head for the refrigerator. As it turns out, nothing in your kitchen can satisfy your hunger pangs anyway. Your longings—like the longings of the man whose life brushed so briefly against mine in the parking lot in New Mexico—stem not from a hunger of the stomach but of the soul.

You already know how the hunger feels: It's the yearning that tugs at your spirit when you stand beneath the stars and realize the universe is vast, that you are small, and that life is ever so short. It's the aching emptiness that descends upon you in the moments when you are alone. It's the nagging sense that something in your world is out of place.

Country singer Tim McGraw claims that this restlessness is "just the cowboy in us all."[1] Truth be told, though, this hunger has nothing to do with the style of your boots or the size of your belt buckle. It's as strong on the coast of Maine as it is on cattle ranches in Montana—or, for that matter, in the clusters of thatched huts that dot the savannahs of Malawi. It's part of the human condition.

Most of the time you're able to consign these cravings to one of the darker corners of your soul. "Though polluted and landlocked by the mighty disaster theologians call the Fall," A. W. Tozer once wrote, "the soul senses its origin and longs to return to its Source."[2] This discontent is what the ancient Hebrew sage must have sensed when he mused, "[God] has planted eternity in the human heart, but even so, people cannot see the whole scope of God's work from beginning to end" (Eccl. 3:11 NLT). These are the silent aches of our souls, the microcosmic echoes of a cosmos that is "groaning in labor pains" (Rom. 8:22). And what all the elements of creation—the planet Mars, the duck-billed platypus, the pulsing currents of the Pacific Ocean, your soul and mine—are groaning for is *glory*. But, somehow, we have convinced ourselves that what we actually need is *more*.

A Beggar with Nothing Written on My Cardboard Sign

Despite our inner groaning for glory, we don't realize that it is glory we're actually craving. We live like beggars with nothing written on our cardboard signs because we don't know what it is we really need. When we live in this way, we become trapped in the spell of television commercials and delusions of self-made success. We swallow the same proposition that Eve embraced as she stood in the center of the garden, never suspecting that the beauty of her nakedness was about to be swept away in a tempest of shame.

What is this proposition?

Simply this: *There's a better life than the one that I'm experiencing right now, and what I need to satisfy my soul is something more than what I already have.*

This proposition is a lie, as it turns out. But it's a lie so powerful and palatable that, more often than I care to admit, I find myself trapped in its deadly embrace.

If the status of my computer's inbox is any indication, so do a lot of other people. Each time I turn on my computer, a new deluge of Internet advertisements tries to convince me of the lie. Just this morning, I deleted two dozen unbeatable deals that promised to provide my family more money than I've ever imagined and to add more inches to a physical feature with which I'm actually quite satisfied. And despite my determination to live in divine glory, there's a seed of doubt planted with each click of the mouse: *Maybe I do need something more than what I have.*

We eventually convince ourselves that perhaps if we surround ourselves with more possessions, we'll be satisfied. As we rack up more debt, we find ourselves working more hours until we have no time to enjoy the very things that were supposed to bring us happiness in the first place. In the end we're left with three-car garages attached to households of two, entertainment systems in every room of the house, closets that bulge with clothes we've never worn, waistlines that bulge with calories we never needed, and souls that remain hungry for something more. "Glory is what we are after," Eugene Peterson writes, "[and] whatever else glory is, it is not just more of what we already have."[3]

And yet we press on, still seeking something more to satisfy our emptiness. In time, we become numb to authentic glory. Brennan Manning states:

> We no longer catch our breath at the sight of a rainbow or the scent of a rose, as we once did.... We no longer run our fingers through water, no longer shout at the stars, or make faces at the moon.... Certainly, the new can amaze us: a space shuttle, the latest computer game, the softest diaper. Till tomorrow, till the new becomes old, till yesterday's wonder is discarded or taken for granted.[4]

One person scours the classified ads in search of a more gratifying career. Another scans an endless series of Internet sites, hoping that the lifeless pixels on his monitor will somehow arrange themselves to reflect more beauty than he has ever seen before. Others push their children to do more, signing them up for sports and school programs and social activities until the delicate beauty of childlike wonder is choked in an endless series of scheduling conflicts. Still others wander into a downtown bar where they discover another variation of this obsession with more. They find that even if they can't quench their inner yearnings, at least they can drown them for a little while. But then the sun rises again and as a throbbing hangover dissolves in the dawning of another day, hunger gnaws anew at the surface of their souls.

The personal proclivities may differ, but the results of this searching remain the same: We find ourselves glutted with superficial pleasures yet still starving for glory. Like the exiled Israelites longing for their lost Land of Promise, we live with "a restless heart, longing eyes, a homesick soul" (Deut. 28:65 MSG). It's as if we're yearning for the familiar scent of a flower whose petals we've never touched, for the latest news from a birthplace whose borders we've never left behind, for the distant melody of a well-known tune that we've never heard before.[5] And, even then, the glory of life waits for a willing heart like a vein of pure gold hidden beneath the riverbed of a soiled stream.

Pornography for the Soul

I'd like to claim that the church provides a refuge from this cultural fixation on seeking more, a shelter from the exchange of authentic glory for an endless tide of more and more hullabaloo. And yet, after more than a decade of pastoral ministry, I've glimpsed a painful truth: Many of the programs I've planned, promoted, and even created haven't led people to embrace the glory already present in their lives. Instead, these programs have reflected and reinforced their frenzied scramble for mor

Suppose some youth have gotten themselves into trouble. The solution suggested by the church's leadership? "The kids need more activities—more things to do to keep them out of trouble." But what if the reason for the students' rash decisions is that they're searching in all the wrong places for the glory that their souls are truly longing for? And what if our many activities simply bury the church's staff under an ever-increasing landslide of to-do lists while leaving the students' spirits empty?

Suppose that the church's attendance is slipping. The proposed solution? "Let's launch some more exciting programs to attract more people!" But what if the reason people aren't showing up is because what they need isn't another exciting program on Sunday but a deeper awareness of God's glory in their lives on Monday?

Suppose the church baptized fewer people this year than last year. Driven by the spiritual psychosis that presumes God's plan is always for our church to become larger than everybody else's—a sort of "steeple envy," I suppose—we respond, "Let's locate a new, improved evangelism program to teach more people how to reach our community!" But what if the people's deepest need isn't one more evangelistic technique? What if the reason the world isn't embracing the gospel is because it has glimpsed a truth to which the church is still blind—the people who claim to be Christians are just as dissatisfied with their lives as non-Christians? And what if the reason Christians are so dissatisfied is that we've assumed our faith is a product designed to satisfy our cultural addiction for more? What if God didn't create us to merely experience *more* hullabaloo? What if he created us instead to experience the glory of life that already hides within the hullabaloo of our present lives?

Despite our apparent convictions to the contrary, more

products and programs—more hullabaloo, in other words—do *not* lead to more glory. Often, they serve to distract from the glory that is present and available in the lives we are already living. Somehow, we seem to have convinced ourselves that some program or curriculum exists to solve every struggle in the Christian life. What's more, the most popular programs claim to solve these struggles in a specific series of predetermined steps.

But what if the emptiness in our souls runs deeper than any series of steps can reach?

What if our persistent fixation on *more*—more programs, more people, more excitement—simply adds another layer of hullabaloo to lives too busy to glimpse the glory that seethes beneath the surface?

What if our churches' many programs are merely pornography for the soul—perversions of God's plan that provide fleeting rushes of pleasure while leaving our true longings unfulfilled? Donald Miller described this dilemma well when he wrote,

> *What is beauty?* I would ask. *Here are the five keys to a successful marriage,* I would be given as an answer. It was as if nobody was listening to the question being groaned by all creation, groaned through the pinings of our sexual tensions, our broken biochemistry, the blending of light and smog to make our glorious sunsets.... [The Christianity I knew] did seem to stem from something beautiful, for sure, but it had been dumbed down and Westernized. If it *was* a religious system that explained the human story, its adherents had lost the grandness of its explanation in exchange for its validation of their *how* lifestyles, to such a degree that the *why* questions seemed to be drowning in the drool of Pavlov's dogs.[6]

According to the apostle Paul, the pagans of past cultures "exchanged the glory of the immortal God for images resembling a mortal human being or birds or four-footed animals or reptiles" (Rom. 1:23). In my own way, I also trade the glory of God for the short-lived pleasures of lesser gods. Where the pagans exchanged divine glory for images of terrestrial beauty, I have substituted one more program, one more series of steps to success, one more hopeless attempt to hush the desperate groaning of my soul.

And the results of this idolatrous exchange?

After studiously memorizing the seven secrets of highly successful people, my résumé still doesn't scream success. After forty days of searching for my purpose, there are still moments when I'm clueless about why God planted me on this planet in the first place. And, after spending several weeks trying to locate my best life now, I'm still stuck with the best life I can manage—and some days, the best life I can manage is trusting the same God when I go to bed that I believed in when I woke up.[7]

Please don't misread my point: I'm not claiming that these series of steps and keys have never helped anyone. What I am suggesting is this: *No product you purchase at your local Christian bookstore and no program your church will ever provide can possibly fill your life with the glory for which you were created.*

There is no program, no pleasure, no series of steps, and no ecstatic experience that can satisfy the deepest cravings of your soul. Only the glory of God can do that. And this glory is not found at the end of a series of steps to success—these steps and keys that add more hullabaloo where there is already plenty. It is found when we embrace the glory that God has already embedded in the hullabaloo of your present life.

Movement Two
Glory in the Hullabaloo, Glory in You

Once, I called you "my God"—
and I could make-believe that your purpose was to meet my needs
because you were my personal deity.
Then, I called you "my King,"
and I could make-believe that I was able to stand beyond life's pain
because I was your royal prince.
But only when I rediscovered the imagination of a child
did I finally discover
who I really am.
I am the child of my heavenly Father.
Nothing more.
Nothing less.
Simply, only, the Father's little boy.
Grimy face, grubby hands
from building my own kingdoms—
they always crumble, mud and sand,
when your glory washes over them.
I didn't like them either,
but your kingdom seemed so far away.
Please, Father, give me your imagination,
the infinite longings of infancy,
that this weathered soul may one day see
the glory that your grace has already
placed in me.

Five

The Real You: Where God's Glory Lives Today—and Where It Doesn't

THE GLORY THAT YOU HAVE GIVEN ME I HAVE GIVEN THEM.

—JESUS OF NAZARETH, JOHN 17:22

YOUR NEW LIFE, WHICH IS YOUR REAL LIFE—EVEN THOUGH INVISIBLE TO SPECTATORS—IS WITH CHRIST IN GOD. HE IS YOUR LIFE. WHEN CHRIST ... SHOWS UP AGAIN ON THIS EARTH, YOU'LL SHOW UP, TOO—THE REAL YOU, THE GLORIOUS YOU."

—THE APOSTLE PAUL, COLOSSIANS 3:3-4 MSG

Some time ago, I decided to spend the day reading Charles Darwin's book *The Descent of Man* in its entirety. I'm not quite certain what power possessed me when I made this decision. I'm not, after all, a fan of Mr. Darwin's ideas, and *The Descent of Man* isn't exactly the most exciting book to grace my shelves.

I suppose the primary reason I decided to read it is precisely because I disagree with Darwin, and it perturbs me when other people punt someone else's ideas without paying attention to what is actually being said in the first place. I think it's a good idea to read what an author says before deciding that his or her ideas have drifted here from the depths of hell. And that's why I spent the better portion of one Friday reading Darwin's book. In the closing chapters, he makes this claim:

> Sexual selection depends on the success of certain individuals over others of the same sex, in relation to the propagation of the species.... The sexual struggle is of two kinds; in the one it is between individuals of the same sex, generally the males, in order to drive away or kill their rivals, the females remaining passive; whilst in the other, the struggle is likewise between the individuals of the same sex, in order to excite or charm those of the opposite sex, generally the females, which no longer remain passive, but select the more agreeable partners.... Man still bears in his bodily frame the indelible stamp of his lowly origin.[1]

If I understand Mr. Darwin correctly, here's what he was getting at: When two people pursue an intimate relationship with each other, it isn't because of love or even lust. All of humanity's capacities for courtship, flirtation, and romance are merely social tools that we have evolved for the sole purpose of preventing the extinction of our personal DNA.

This seems logical—but is it really true?

I wonder if Charles Darwin really believed this. I mean, did Darwin ever say to his wife, "You know, honey, the only reason I married you is because you seemed like the best choice for passing on my genetic code"? If Darwin did say anything of the sort, I can almost guarantee you that he spent many cold nights sleeping alone.

Here's what I suspect, though: Deep inside, in moments of passion, even Charles Darwin knew something more was happening than his desire to keep his DNA from following the dinosaurs down the pathway to extinction. There is magic and wonder and mystery in this mysterious intertwining of man and woman—something that defies scientific explanation.

Every human being already knows this. It isn't shame or repression that causes first-graders to share their sexual misinformation with each other in such hushed tones. It's the instinctive awareness that this mysterious country on whose borders they so gingerly tread is a sacred place—a place where God has breathed a reflection of his own glory. Wasn't that the point Moses was trying to make in the opening chapter of Genesis? He wrote, "God created humankind in his image, … male and female he created them.… God said to them, 'Be fruitful and multiply'" (Gen. 1:27–28).

And yet, in the shadow of the scientific revolution, the temptation remains to reduce human sexuality to a logical process of surefire steps: *Join Part A with Part B while in contact with Part C, repeating* … Sure, this may work on paper, but who wants to share life's most intimate moments with someone who's making a list and checking it twice? Yet, scientists and researchers have continued to reduce relationships to measurable quantities: How large? How long? How many times? All the while, the human soul starves for something more profound than any caliper can calculate. The full wonder of the relationship is greater and more mysterious than any physical process or series of steps. What humanity craves isn't greater biological ecstasy but to know and to be known in nakedness of the flesh and vulnerability of the soul. They have sold us the lie that everything that really matters can be clocked and counted and reenacted in control groups.

I've heard the results of this reduction while counseling hundreds of discontented couples: "If only my spouse were more like *this,*" one partner or the other claims, "then I'd be happy." And what they seem to want from me is a series of steps to follow to make them happier. But, even if one of them did suddenly become more romantic, more attractive, or more industrious, it wouldn't set their relationship on the highway to happiness. Their souls are frustrated because they have reduced their relationship to a search for some ecstatic experience or series of steps they are trusting to bring them happiness.

I think this is why the Christian faith as I knew it frustrated me for so many years.

I can still see the tracts with which I littered thousands of porches as a preteen, providing anyone willing to pray the preprinted prayer with a ticket into heaven. There was a pink and grey one called "God's Simple Plan of Salvation," a blue one with white lettering that read, "God Loves You and Has a Wonderful Plan for Your Life," and a miniature comic book with the words "This Was Your Life" emblazoned in red across the cover. They were cheaply printed and left dark streaks on my fingertips as I stuffed them into the dark space between each door and its frame, praying at each house that the people inside would turn from their sins. Or maybe I was just praying that I would run out of tracts quickly so I could get home in time to watch the latest *Transformers* cartoon. I don't really remember anymore.

All these scraps of paper were created with good intentions, each one calculated in its own way to increase the number of people entering into God's kingdom. And yet each one shrank the infinite mystery of God into a series of laws or steps or poorly rendered comic strips. *Admit this, believe that, repeat this prayer after me, and*—bingo—*you've made it off the naughty list*. The process described in each tract had the capacity, supposedly, to satisfy the deepest desires of the human soul, but where is the glory in worshipping a God who's merely making a list and checking it twice? Simply put, these tracts did to divine glory what *The Descent of Man* did to the relationship of a woman and man: They twisted and truncated an infinitely glorious mystery into a sequence of rational steps.

It seems to me that Christians do this often. It's as if we try to capture every experience of divine glory and turn it into a program or curriculum. Suppose that a work of God erupts in a particular church. This glorious movement of God is mysterious and miraculous—probably a unique work of God, specifically given to this church. Yet, within a few months, church-growth experts have analyzed this movement of God and reduced it to a series of steps so that other church leaders can implement it in their own congregations. Publishers bind these principles in books and box them in curricula, and these principles become the authoritative paradigms for thousands of congregations. Some of these churches experience divine glory, and some don't. But, for the ones that didn't happen to catch the glory the first time around, there's always the live worship CD, inspired by the principles described in the curriculum, which is guaranteed to provide that final push into the life of glory.

The motivation for all of this seems pure: Christian companies want more people to experience these glimpses of God's work, so they turn them into products that anyone can purchase. And, to be sure, some of these products are helpful.

But what if our constant focus on experiencing glory through products and programs actually distracts us from the glory that is available in each present moment of life? Suppose the most glorious examples of God's work can't be reduced to a program or transferred from place to place at our whim. Suppose our souls are seeking something greater than anything that can be typeset in a tract and lovelier than anything that can fit into a prepackaged curriculum. Suppose that the exit ramp marked "more" never leads to a life of glory.

As I have considered these possibilities, I've found some comfort in the fact that the Christians of the current generations aren't the first band of believers to be torn between authentic glory and a fixation on our culture's obsession with more.

Remember the church in Corinth?

When Paul penned his letters to the Corinthians in the middle of the first century, some of the Corinthians had bought into their own culture's fixation on more. One group in Corinth claimed that what they really needed was a more ecstatic spiritual experience (1 Cor. 14:1–25). Others were searching for more eloquent teachers—at first, it was Apollos of Alexandria, then the so-called "super-apostles" (Acts 18:24—19:1; 1 Cor. 1:12; 3:4; 2 Cor. 11:5; 12:11). Still others tried to hush the groaning of their souls with one more gulp of wine, one more mouthful of food, one more forbidden sexual encounter (1 Cor. 5:1; 6:12–20; 11:21). And yet, their souls remained frustrated, starving for something more—so frustrated, in fact, that they weren't even able to live in peace with one another (1 Cor. 3:3–4).

And it wasn't only after Jesus vanished through a gaping gash in the Judean sky that his followers developed these tendencies. Remember the words of Simon Peter on the Mount of Transfiguration? Standing before God the Son in unveiled glory, conversing with Moses and Elijah, Peter glimpsed the glory that his soul had craved for so long.

"Master," Peter cried out, "this is a great moment! Let's build three memorials: one for you, one for Moses, and one for Elijah" (Luke 9:33 MSG). In other words, "Let's enshrine this experience of glory into a three-step program—the perfect solution for fulfilling the deepest desires of the human soul!"

And what was God's response?

"Great idea, Peter! *Never* could I have come up with that by myself. Maybe we can package it up and market it to every synagogue in the Roman Empire. If we don't emphasize suffering and persecution too much, maybe a few pagan temples will even purchase the curriculum!"

Not even close.

"This is my Son, the Chosen!" heaven thundered in reply, "Listen to him!" (Luke 9:35 MSG). Which is to say, "Stuff it, Peter. You don't understand what you're talking about."

So, what was God's problem? Why didn't Simon's plans to preserve God's glory receive a heavenly seal of approval? Even if three shrines couldn't contain *all* of God's splendor, wouldn't it have been nice to have a spot on some picturesque mountain peak where anyone could catch a glimpse of glory divine? Why didn't God want his glory enshrined in this place?

Why God Wouldn't Let His Glory Live in a Tent

A plain answer to this question didn't come until near the end of the Messiah's time on planet Earth. In fact, it became clear just a few moments before Jesus was betrayed in the garden. Traveling up the western slope of the Mount of Olives, Jesus said to his Father, "The glory that you have given me I have given them" (John 17:22).

Did you catch that?

"The glory that you have given me *I have given them.*"

The reason God didn't want his glory enshrined on a mountain was because he had a greater plan. (He usually does, you know. It's one of the many perquisites of being God.) God's plan was for the glory that Simon Peter wanted to entrench in a trio of tents to be present in Peter's very soul.

And Simon Peter wasn't the only one who was destined to get in on this deal. "The glory which you have given me," Jesus whispered, "I have given *them.*"

"Them," he said.

This pronoun potentially included Simon Peter and the rest of the disciples, but it didn't stop there. According to Jesus, it embraces everyone "who will believe in me because of them and their witness about me" (John 17:20 MSG).

Do you know whom that includes?

Me.

Yes, *me*—and, if you've entrusted your life to Jesus, *you.*

Inasmuch as I am a follower of Jesus, the same glory that filled the life of Jesus is present right here, right now, in my life. The glory that hurled the prophets to their knees, the glory that Israel's offspring could not bear to see, the glory that shined in the face of the man from Galilee—that glory is present in you and me (Ex. 20:18–19; Isa. 6:1–5; John 1:14).

So, why didn't Jesus didn't want to place his glory in the tent that Simon Peter had planned? Because he wanted to place his glory in *us* instead. "The glory which you have given me," he said, "I have given to them." And, indeed, he has. The reason this glory is too beautiful to enshrine on a mountaintop and too vast to fit into a boxed curriculum at your local Christian bookstore is because God designed this glory to be poured into *you*.

Finding the Real You

Despite his initial dim-wittedness, Simon Peter eventually grasped this truth. "The spirit of glory, which is the Spirit of God, is resting on you," Peter later said to some of his friends in the midst of their persecution (1 Peter 4:14). Another apostle, Paul, made the point even more clearly: "Your new life, which is your real life—even though invisible to spectators—is with Christ in God. He is your life. When Christ ... shows up again on this earth, you'll show up, too—the real you, the glorious you" (Col. 3:3–4 MSG).[2]

Do you know what I think Paul was getting at in these verses?

Remember how resplendent Moses, Elijah, and Jesus looked on the mountain?

That's how "the real you, the glorious you" looks all the time.

The *real you* isn't the rapidly wrinkling face that stared back at you from the mirror this morning. The *real you* isn't the failure-prone person who never seems to lose enough weight or gain enough confidence to become what you've always dreamed. The *real you* isn't the sum of your many frailties and fears.

The *real you* is already resting in heavenly places with Jesus himself (Eph. 2:6).

The *real you* is forever being transfigured from one degree of glory to another (2 Cor. 3:18).

The *real you* shines like the brightest star (Dan. 12:3).

The *real you* is stunningly beautiful.

The *real you* is infinitely glorious.

And when your heavenly Father looks at you, do you know what he sees?

That's right—*the real you.*

To be sure, the rest of humanity probably won't glimpse this glorious identity until "Christ ... is revealed" at the end of time (Col. 3:4). Yet, this truth remains: Through Jesus Christ, the glory of God the Father has become your glory. When your Father looks at you, he sees glory.

So, what does this truth mean for your day-to-day life? If indeed the Spirit of Glory lives within you at this moment, you can release your persistent pursuit of something better, something greater, something more than you possess right now. You already possess everything that your soul is starving for. The glory your soul craves is present in you.

Don't get me wrong: I'm not claiming that there is nothing in your life that needs to change. What I am suggesting is that everything you need to make these changes is obtainable in your present life, though it may take some pointed questions from a trusted friend or counselor to unmask these epic possibilities.

In some cases, achieving these possibilities may require a difficult choice or two—changes in your lifestyle, transformation of your attitudes, perhaps even something from your doctor to help you perceive your life's events more objectively. However, if the Spirit of Glory is present in your life, everything you need to make these changes and experience God's glory is available to you in the context of the life that you're already living.

This glorious life doesn't fit into any logical sequence or preprogrammed curriculum. It is not a goal you can achieve by enrolling in one more program or devouring one more book. The life of glory is a gift you receive by coming to grips with the glory that is already available here and now.

This means that you can stop running from one program to another, looking for the answers to your life's difficulties. There is no life greater than the one God is offering to you right now, and there is no moment more glorious than the one you are experiencing right now.

That's what it means to have "the spirit of glory … resting on you" (1 Peter 4:14).

Six

Imagination: Why Children Hold the Title Deed to God's Kingdom

I'M TELLING YOU, ONCE AND FOR ALL, THAT UNLESS YOU RETURN TO SQUARE ONE AND START OVER LIKE CHILDREN, YOU'RE NOT EVEN GOING TO GET A LOOK AT THE KINGDOM, LET ALONE GET IN.

—JESUS OF NAZARETH, MATTHEW 18:3 MSG

IT MAY NOT BE AUTOMATIC NECESSITY THAT MAKES ALL DAISIES ALIKE; IT MAY BE THAT GOD MAKES EVERY DAISY SEPARATELY, BUT HAS NEVER GOT TIRED OF MAKING THEM. IT MAY BE THAT HE HAS THE ETERNAL APPETITE OF INFANCY; FOR WE HAVE SINNED AND GROWN OLD, AND OUR FATHER IS YOUNGER THAN WE.

—G. K. CHESTERTON, ORTHODOXY

At this point, perhaps you're wondering, "All this talk about glory sounds great—but *how?* How is God's glory present in the hullabaloo of my life? And how can I possibly live every moment in this glory?"

Well, I recently came up with a simple, six-step plan that my publisher has guaranteed will not only enable you to live in God's glory but also eliminate frigid showers forever by miraculously increasing the capacity of your water heater.

No, wait, that's the other book I'm writing—the one that's destined to become the paradigmatic curriculum for millions of American churches.

In this book there are no steps that lead inevitably to a life of glory. Instead, there is this single truth: *Everything you need to live a life of glory is hidden in the hullabaloo of the life that you're already living.* If Jesus Christ is present in you, then you can live here and now with the assurance that your life is already filled with glory (see Col. 1:27).[1]

And, yet, the question remains: "*How?* How do I learn to find this glory in every moment of my life?"

A Better Imagination

In the past few years, I have made some progress when it comes to glimpsing glory in the hullabaloo. But I must confess something: Despite my passionate convictions about the presence of divine glory in my day-to-day life, there are still moments when I find myself ambling through the aisles of a bookstore or wandering the twisted mazes of the World Wide Web, searching for some future possibility to solve my present longing for glory.

Of course it's possible there's a glitch unique to my soul

that causes me to forget the nearness of God's glory. Perhaps a sense of God's closeness comes easily to you. Maybe you're less like me and more like the woman who, at this moment, is seated two tables away from me at an exurban coffee shop. She has spent the past half hour recounting her most recent spiritual experiences to her reverential companion. Thus far, I have learned that Jesus has personally revealed to this woman reasons that the United States should launch all-out war on the Palestinians, when her Mary Kay business will finally prove profitable (somehow this relates to the Palestinian issue, but I must have dozed off when she explained the precise connection), and how Jesus will avenge the years that she wasted on her ex-husband. Jesus most often tells her these things while she's jogging.

Somehow, Jesus and I never seem to have those sorts of conversations.

The only epiphany I've experienced while jogging is that I need to exercise more.

Yet, as I listen to the undertones of this woman's conversation, I sense that she too craves something more than what these revelations have provided. Her supposed inside information about God's workings may have satisfied the outward curiosities of her mind. Yet her inward rage and irritation reveal a deeper truth—her soul is still dissatisfied.

More often than I care to admit, so is mine.

I'd like to think that I'm alone in my failures, but the frustration on the faces of my fellow believers tells me I'm not. I deal daily with people who feel too busy, too guilty, too stressed, or simply too tired to embrace the glory their souls so deeply crave. As I work with them, I wish I possessed some sort of magical key guaranteed by God to open the floodgates of divine glory in every believer's present life.

But I have no such key.

I have no series of surefire steps and no hidden secrets of spiritual success. Despite the clamoring to the contrary that seems to have contaminated contemporary Christian thinking—"Follow these steps, and God is guaranteed to bless you with abundant wealth and healing"—neither does anyone else.

What I do have is this fragment of truth drawn from one of those points at which my reading of the Scriptures has fused with the experiences of my life: *When I am able to glimpse the glimmerings of glory in the hullabaloo of my daily life, it is most often because I have recovered—if only for a moment—a childlike imagination.*

Are you failing to glimpse the glory in your present life?

Maybe what you need is a better imagination.

Yes, *imagination.*

But not just any imagination.

What you need to recover is your sense of childlike wonder—a sense that you may have left behind about the same time as teddy bears and bedtime storybooks.

What you need is the imagination of a child.

Capturing a Childlike Imagination

Once, when Jesus' first followers were bickering about which of them was most likely to succeed his Master, the Messiah silenced them with this comment: "I'm telling you, once and for all, that unless you return to square one and start over like children, you're not even going to get a look at the kingdom, let alone get in" (Matt. 18:3 MSG).

At one time I thought Jesus meant that children were naturally pure and good. Understood in this way, Jesus was informing the disciples that if they planned to catch sight of God's kingdom, they needed to recapture the goodness and purity of a little child.[2]

Then I became a parent.

Don't get me wrong; I adore my daughter. She is the apple of my eye, the princess of my heart, and whenever she lures me down the aisles of Limited Too, the depleter of my checking account.

But she is *not* naturally good.

Truth be told, my child is evil.

At this moment Hannah is defeating my wife in a game of chess. I watch my daughter's expressions of malevolent glee as she eliminates opposing rooks and pawns. As I glimpse this child's merciless calculations, I recognize a dismal truth: Left to herself, my daughter will grow up to be the ruthless despot of some poor, volatile nation in the third world. While other fathers are recounting how their offspring have recently completed degrees in medicine and law, I will be talking about my child's latest military coup. Barely veiled beneath this girl's adorable brown curls, there is the brain of a brutal tyrant. And it all started because I thought it would be a good idea for her to learn to play chess.

Okay, so maybe my daughter won't actually become the dictator of any domain much larger than her daddy's heart. But, apart from parental discipline Hannah would tell the truth only when it's convenient, complete her homework only when it's easy, and cooperate with other children only when they do things her way. "I was," the royal psalmist lamented as he stood in the shadow of his own moral failures, "born a sinner—yes, from the moment my mother conceived me" (Ps. 51:5 NLT). So was my child—and so was everyone else's.

So, if becoming "like a child" isn't about becoming pure or good, what *is* it about?

The primary focus of Jesus' words was probably based on the fact that under the Roman principle of *patria potestas,* children in the ancient world had no power and no rights apart from the will of their fathers.[3] But I think Jesus was also hinting at something else when he told his disciples to become like children: *children imagine glory where the rest of humanity sees garbage.*[4] Frederick Buechner captured this truth with characteristic eloquence when he wrote,

> When the disciples, overearnest as ever, asked Jesus who was the greatest in the Kingdom of Heaven, Jesus pulled a child out of the crowd and said the greatest in the Kingdom of Heaven were people like this.... They are people who, like children, are so relatively unburdened by preconceptions that if somebody says there's a pot of gold at the end of the rainbow, they are perfectly willing to go take a look for themselves.[5]

Spend some time playing with children whose imaginations haven't been drowned in a deluge of television commercials, and you too will sense the boundless optimism of a child's heart. Quests of epic proportions occur amid the simplest of objects. Broken branches miraculously transform into fearsome swords, cast-off cardboard cartons become grandiose castles, and sticky clods of dirt can be dolloped onto cracked plates to produce banquets fit for a king. Unfettered by the awful pride of thinking that they know precisely where glory is present, children still imagine glorious possibilities where the rest of us see only rubbish. Simply put, children can still see glory in the hullabaloo.

Eugene Peterson writes,

> When we were children, we were in a constant state of wonder—the world was new, tumbling in on us in profusion. We staggered through each day fondling, looking, tasting. Words were wondrous. Running was wondrous. Touch, taste, sound. We lived in a world of wonders. We became Christians and found to our delight … that the wonder is deep and eternal, that we are part of a creation that is "very good." But gradually a sense of wonder gets squeezed out of us.[6]

The moments when I glimpse glory in the hullabaloo are the moments when I recover—if only for a moment—this childlike "sense of wonder."

The Eternal Appetite of Infancy

I think that's why Jesus was so adamant about childlikeness in his followers. "Let the children alone, don't prevent them from coming to me," he told his disciples when they tried to clear urchins and orphans from their rabbi's daily agenda. "God's kingdom is made up of people like these" (Matt. 19:14 MSG). Put another way, *God's kingdom is the property of people who can still imagine glory in the people and events that the rest of the world counts as garbage.*

Why?

Because that's what God imagines.

The more I read the Scriptures, the more I become convinced that, at the core of his being, God is an infinite dreamer, a tenacious romantic, a cosmic idealist with the boundless imagination of a child. God looks within the hubbub and hullabaloo of human existence—into the very places where the world sees only rubbish—and imagines glory. Wasn't that Paul's point when he penned these words to the Corinthian church?

> Consider your own call, brothers and sisters: not many of you were wise by human standards, not many were powerful, not many were of noble birth. But God chose what is foolish in the world to shame the wise; God chose what is weak in the world to shame the strong. (1 Cor. 1:26–27)

God chooses the so-called garbage—what the world views as "foolish" and "weak," ordinary and monotonous—to reveal his presence to us. Yet God never becomes bored with the apparent monotony of revealing his glory through ordinary (and even less-than-ordinary) people and events. And why not? *Because God possesses the imagination to see the hidden glory in each one.*

Viewed in this way, our heavenly Father lives with the heart of a child, bursting eternally with the boundless imagination of youth. In his classic work *Orthodoxy*, G. K. Chesterton mused,

> Children … always say, "Do it again"; and the grown-up person does it again until he is nearly dead. For grown-up people are not strong enough to exult in monotony. But perhaps God is strong enough to exult in monotony. It is possible that God says every morning, "Do it again" to the sun; and every evening, "Do it again" to the moon. It may not be automatic necessity that makes all daisies alike; it may be that God makes

> every daisy separately, but has never got tired of making them. It may be that he has the eternal appetite of infancy; for we have sinned and grown old, and our Father is younger than we.[7]

So, how do we develop the imagination to see the hidden glory around us? How can we regain the wonder of childhood? What is it that keeps us from living with "the eternal appetite for infancy"?

The Problem with the Block Party

Somewhere on the pathway between infancy and adulthood, it seems that we become suspicious of the world around us—with good reason, I suppose. In this world there are people that want to hurt us and sicknesses that could kill us. Hearts break, relationships wither, automobiles are hurled into one another with deathly violence, and airplanes plunge into flower-dotted fields from clear blue skies. "This is a world where robins die, and sparrows, and people: the ones we love, the ones Jesus loves.... They fall to the ground, they are enfolded into the earth. And most times, Jesus doesn't come to raise them up, not in our lifetime, not so that we see."[8] In such a place it's easy to become suspicious of the world around us.

This worldly-wise, grown-up suspicion protects us from harm, to be sure, but it also suffocates any sense of childlike wonder. Living in suspicion, we lose the capacity to believe that something that's too good to be true might actually *be* true. For those who want to live with the imagination of a child, this capacity is essential.

The first time I glimpsed this truth, I was walking through a neighborhood park where, in the shadow of slides and jungle gyms, prostitutes picked up their johns, dealers exchanged moments of empty pleasure for fistfuls of cash, and drunks choked on their own vomit. A community relief agency in East St. Louis had planned a spring block party with free games and food, toilet paper and soap, and even kitchen appliances for anyone that showed up. The idea was that when families came for the free items, counselors would be available to enroll the adults in reading classes, rehabilitation programs, and job training.

A week before the party, a team from our church and I found ourselves wandering the streets on an afternoon in late March, handing out flyers. The entire neighborhood reeked of desperation. House after house, duct tape and chipboard had replaced glass panes in the weatherworn window frames. Doors dangled unevenly from broken hinges, and termite-ridden steps lurched precariously whenever we placed our weight on them. Occasionally, above the ragged roofs, I glimpsed the gleaming grandeur of the Gateway Arch—a monument of hope towering just beyond this matrix of despair.

Within a few minutes, it became clear that something was going terribly wrong with our mission. The children took the flyers with joy, asking, "Really? It *all* be free?" before skipping toward their homes, clutching pink papers in their fists.

With a few exceptions, the adults didn't respond so readily.

In fact, some of the adults seemed angry.

"What you doin' here?" a middle-aged man asked as he looked at the flyer, then hurled it into a storm drain. "What kinda fools you takin' us for? Go back ta y' home!"

Then a mother yelled through a broken window, "Ain't you

got no respect for my kids? Don't you go messin' with their hopes! Why you tryin' to make fools out of us?"

Two houses later, as I skirted the edge of the neighborhood park, it finally occurred to me what was happening. The problem was the date of the block party printed in huge letters at the top of each flyer.

It was April 1.

It hadn't occurred to anyone that the projected date was April Fools' Day.

In the shadow of a lifetime of shattered dreams, the adults thought we were playing a joke—a sick prank. It was as if they couldn't imagine they were actually being invited to a party of this sort—a party where everything they needed was free. It seemed too good to be true, and no claims to the contrary could convince them otherwise. Suspicion had squelched any sense of childlike wonder from their souls. But the children accepted this news with squeals of delight. Perhaps it was because the children hadn't heard of April Fools' Day, or maybe it was because the children still believed that something too good to be true might actually *be* true.

The remaining flyers went directly into the hands of children. And a week later when the community center opened its doors on April 1, guess who walked away with hot dogs, snow cones, and armloads of groceries? You guessed it—children. The grown-ups missed the party because they thought it was too good to be true.

I miss the glory of life for the same reason.

Too often, I look at my life with grown-up suspicion, and the thought that infinite glory might be present in my life here and now seems too good to be true. In these moments, I feel as though God's failure to immediately respond to my prayers implies that he's forgotten me. I suspect that other people like me less because of the clothes I wear, the house I own, or the car I drive. I wonder, *If only I weighed less or worked harder or made more money, maybe then I would find what I'm looking for.* In my suspicion, I lose sight of the truth: All the joy I need—all the glory that my heart craves—is already available to me in the life I am presently living.

To live with the imagination of a child is to let go of our suspicion; it is to believe that, if God is truly our Father, there is more glory in our lives than darkness, more splendor than spite, more goodness than death. It is to begin to believe that the things that are too good to be true might actually *be* true.

Learning to Live Free

Suppose, just for a moment, that you *did* let go of your suspicion? What if you regained the imagination of a child—the capacity to imagine glory in every segment of your life? What about the time you spend waiting in morning traffic, impatient with your circumstances and frustrated with your fellow drivers? Could it be that these moments are bursting with glories unseen? The sun slowly lifting its head over the eastern horizon, distant trees with limbs stretched upward like eager fingers straining to caress the sky, droplets of dew sliding across your windshield, the saltless tears of a planet that still groans for redemption—all of them, fingerprints of divine splendor, unnoticed because the search for glory is not on that day's agenda.

What if you honestly allowed the search for glory to form the way you responded to every person you encountered? Coworkers and cashiers, mechanics and metalworkers, tollbooth operators and teachers? What if you responded to each of them—though they may be unaware of it—as though divine glory pulses beneath the surface of their daily lives as well? If it is in God that we each "live and move and have our being," then there must be echoes of glory in them, too. After all, we live in a world where saints, prophets, angels, and even God himself have shown up in the least likely of packages. Why, then, is it so unimaginable that glory itself might be hanging out in your neighborhood, dispensing change and changing diapers?

What if you fully embraced the truth that God places his glorious treasures "in jars of clay"—in the people and places that seem the least resplendent (2 Cor. 4:7 NIV)? What if you released your suspicion and learned to live with the imagination of a child, constantly glimpsing the glistering of glory in the hullabaloo of your daily living?

Guess what?

You can.

If the Spirit of Glory lives within you, there is no reason you cannot imagine glory in every segment of your life—no reason beyond or besides your own choice to see what God sees when he looks at the world.

Think about it: What might change if you could see what God sees in the world around you?

I think I know.

You would become *free*—free to allow infinite glory to fill the emptiness in your soul, free to spill this glory into the lives of others, free to live in childlike faith, free to give away anything you possess, free to ignore the commercials that correlate your happiness with your buying habits, free to rejoice in the hints of your Savior's presence in every part of your life. "Wherever the Spirit of the Lord is," the apostle Paul commented to the Corinthians, "he gives freedom, … so that we can be mirrors that brightly reflect the glory of the Lord. And as the Spirit of the Lord works within us, we become more and more like him and reflect his glory even more" (2 Cor. 3:17–18 NLT).

That's what it means to live with the imagination of a child.

Seven

Control: Why You Still Stink at Following Jesus

All of life is a pure gift.

—Henri Nouwen, *The Return of the Prodigal Son*

Give thanks in all circumstances, for this is God's will for you in Christ Jesus.

—The Apostle Paul
1 Thessalonians 5:18 NIV

A few months ago, our church struck a minor rough spot: An unintended miscommunication hurt a committee member's feelings, hurt feelings led to harsh words, and harsh words led to more hurt feelings. In the end everything worked out. Yet, in retrospect, I realized the associate pastor and I could have handled the situation much better.

Our lack of foresight is the reason that a few weeks later, Jeremy and I found ourselves standing in the parking lot of Mimi's Café after lunch, trying to figure out the best way to deal with the fallout. Both of us, in our own way, had reacted without thinking about what God might be doing in this situation. Apologies were in order, and we knew it. This wouldn't have been such a big deal if Jesus hadn't offered such annoying advice about these issues. Here's what he said to his first followers:

> I'm telling you that anyone who is so much as angry with a brother or sister is guilty of murder.... If you enter your place of worship, and ... you suddenly remember a grudge a friend has against you, ... go to this friend and make things right. Then and only then, come back and work things out with God. (Matt. 5:22–24 MSG)

Being told to live like this is quite irritating, if you want to know the truth, especially when Jesus is so earnest about it that, well, it's almost as if he expects us to take him seriously.

And yet Jeremy and I both felt obligated to take Jesus seriously; we're *pastors,* after all. Taking Jesus seriously is probably in our job descriptions, somewhere near the section about severance pay.

A moment of silence descended on the two of us after

we had batted back and forth for a while about what the possible responses might be. There we stood staring at the sidewalk, grinding bits of fresh-mown grass into green-tinged fragments beneath our sandaled feet.

"You know," Jeremy finally said, "sometimes I really stink at following Jesus."

I deliberated for a moment as I watched waves of heat rise from the sea of cars and concrete that surrounded us. I'd never really thought of it that way before, but I realized I felt the same way.

"Yeah," I replied after some time, "Me too. We all do, I guess."

And I realized that it was true. After all these years of studying the Scriptures and claiming the title "Christian," I still wasn't an expert at following Jesus. Once in a while I could convince myself that I was doing quite well at following Jesus—no outstanding sins, cordial relations with most of my fellow believers, studying the Bible nearly every day.

But in the blunt honesty of this moment I saw how far I still fell short of following Jesus.

In Jesus I saw someone who became a slave for the sake of his Father's plan, who looked at every person with childlike imagination, who saw his Father's glory in every sliver of the hullabaloo—in the fall of a common sparrow, in the call of a few fishermen, in lilies and lepers, in grubby children, in the agony of a cross.

And what about the successes in my spiritual life—the ones that so quickly become sources of pride? In the shadow of the cross, they are nothing. What about the petty pleasures that so easily distract me? In the shadow of the cross, they are foolishness.

I still stink at following Jesus.

One of the academic degrees I've earned is the "Master of Divinity"—in other words, an expert in the things of God.

What an idiotic name for a degree.

This piece of paper on my wall arrogantly claims that I've achieved some sort of mastery when it comes to experiencing God.

This is a lie.

I am no master of the things of God. I am a pilgrim struggling—and frequently failing—to allow the things of God to master me. I am no expert at following Jesus. This is especially true when it comes to looking at the hullabaloo with the imagination of a child. Even at my best, my capacity to glimpse glory in every part of my life falls far short of Jesus' example. He lived as if all the glory he needed was already available in him and around him in every moment of his life. I am making progress in living like he did, but there are still moments when I find myself caught up in the frenzied struggle for more.

But why?

Why can't I see splendor in the hullabaloo like Jesus did? Why don't I look at every part of my life with childlike imagination? Why do I still perform so poorly when it comes to following Jesus?

Those questions simmered in my mind for several weeks after that afternoon in the parking lot. I even talked to God about it. And yesterday I think I received some semblance of an answer. I'm quite certain this answer is the truth, but I must confess it wasn't really the answer I wanted.

The Problem with Talking to God

Yesterday was Secretary's Day. I had planned to meet my secretary and the rest of the church's staff at El Tequila's, an upscale Mexican joint. We have an outstanding secretary without whom the associate pastor and I would most likely spend our days wandering the church halls, wondering what we're supposed to be doing, then going to lunch at random times—perhaps several times in the same day. Actually, this is what we do anyway, but the secretary covers for us so well that hardly anyone notices. That's why, in addition to taking her to lunch, we had picked up flowers, gift certificates, movie tickets, and a candle in a fancy box. Jeremy and I hoped these offerings would convince Lily to put up with us for at least another year.

Somehow, despite my best-laid plans, I mixed up the directions to the restaurant and ended up halfway across Tulsa from my intended location. I do this quite often, to tell you the truth.

After three telephone calls, I got my directions straight.

Then, my car and a locomotive needed to cross the same railroad tracks at the same time. I noticed that the train was considerably larger than my Mustang, so I let the locomotive go first.

And then my low fuel light began to blink.

In case you ever need to know, pounding the steering wheel while cursing does not automatically fill up your fuel tank. It also doesn't make trains move faster. Nor does it speed up farm vehicles cruising along at a whopping fifteen miles per hour on hilly, two-lane roads. Nor make traffic lights turn green. It does, however, provoke unusual and interesting expressions on the faces of other drivers.

By now, I was *really* late.

The hullabaloo wasn't flowing so well for me.

At this point, I made a mistake: I talked to God about it. Talking to God is typically a great idea—but only if you're willing to be changed. At this moment, I had no desire to change. What

I wanted was someone to validate my feelings, to place a stamp of approval on my frustrations.

If you want someone to validate your feelings so you can feel better about a rotten attitude, talk to your psychotherapist, your dog, or your pillow. If you're particularly desperate, talk to your cat—but don't talk to God. God's patience with self-centered attitudes is amazingly brief.

"God!" the word tore across my tongue in a staccato burst. "Why can't things work out according to the plans I've made? Why do I always end up in situations that make me so mad?"

Because, a silent whisper slipped from somewhere deeper than my soul, *you still want to be in control of every circumstance. But you're not in control, and you're not supposed to be. You're acting as if your anger can change things, but it never has, and it never will.*

Maybe not, my mind retorted, *but it makes me feel better.*

No, the inaudible whisper returned, *it doesn't.*

And the whisper was right.

The primary reason I fail to see the same glory in my life that Jesus saw in his is simply this: I still want to live under the delusion that I should control the hullabaloo. I wanted to manipulate the traffic, the train, my staff members' perceptions of their pastor, and no matter how angry I became, I could not control any of them. Then, instead of embracing what God might be doing in the hullabaloo, I simply became angrier.

I don't know if it was God or me that manufactured this momentary epiphany, but whoever it was saw the dark truth about the inner workings of my soul.

I want to be in control of the hullabaloo.

When I can't control my circumstances, I become frustrated and angry. However, the only thing my frustrations have ever changed is me, and the changes have never been good. They've never even made me feel better. The changes in me have sent my blood pressure uphill and my awareness of God's glory downhill, but they've never reversed the events that triggered my frustration in the first place. Believing that my anger can change the hullabaloo is like believing that I can obliterate the sun by blinding myself. It may feel as though I have destroyed my adversary, but, in truth, all that I have done is destroy myself (see James 1:19–20).[1]

This is why I stink at seeing the glory in the hullabaloo. But, ever so slowly, that's beginning to change.

The Grand Delusion

What I've realized is that I have lived most of my life captivated by the delusion that I should be in control. It's a stupid delusion to be sure, but much of the time it's also a quite pleasant one. When I embrace the delusion that I should be in control, I live assuming that if I plan well and follow the right steps, the hullabaloo of my life will always move me toward places of prosperity and peace. And if I don't happen to know the right steps, surely there's some new best seller in the self-help section that will point me in the right direction.

This is, of course, the pattern of life that the ancient prophets called "idolatry"—the belief that I can control my future and that something besides God can fill my soul with glory. When I live under this delusion, my heart becomes, in the words of a sixteenth-century theologian named John Calvin, "a perpetual factory of idols."[2] And, somehow, idolatry and divine glory have never developed the capacity to play well together. "My people have exchanged their Glory for worthless idols," God bellows through the prophet Jeremiah. "Be appalled at this, O heavens, and shudder with great horror" (Jer. 2:11–12 NIV). God makes much the same point through another prophet, Isaiah: "I will not give my glory to anyone else. I will not share my praise with carved idols" (Isa. 42:8 NIV). In other words, "The life of glory will never be a commodity you can control."

For some reason, God has no respect for the delusion that I should be in control. After all these years he still insists that the top spot in the universe belongs to him.

Why They Make Electric Blankets with Dual Controls

When I live under the delusion that I should be in control, I clearly see the splendor of my own plans for my future. This splendor, though, is a false glory, an idolatrous imitation of divine splendor.

Only when I release this delusion do I begin to glimpse the infinite glory that God has poured into the life I am presently living—a glory that is eternal and real (2 Cor. 4:17).

But releasing this delusion isn't easy—it isn't for me, anyway.

Like a man desperately clinging to a defective parachute as he plummets to the earth beneath him, I find myself refusing to let go of the futile delusion that I should be in control. Most of the rest of humanity must shop at the same store as me because everyone else seems to have a similar notion about himself or herself. The problem is that everyone in the universe can't be in charge at the same time. That's why we live in a world filled with failed political summits, misguided wars, road rage, electric blankets with dual controls, and televisions in every room of the house. Everyone wants to be in control.

So, where does this delusion come from?

This delusion is, it seems, as deep as the human heart and as ancient as the primal rebellion against God. If you don't believe me, look at some of the Hebrew people's most venerable stories: Slithering amid the leaves of Eden, the serpent suggested to Eve, "You will be like God" (Gen. 3:5). In other words, "You can be in control." Brandishing a bloodied club over his brother's lifeless body, Cain felt a fleeting rush of satisfaction, because—if only for an instant—the first murderer felt as if he could control life and death (Gen. 4:1–12). A few decades after Noah's flood, humanity stood on the cornerstone of the Tower of Babel and cried out, "Come, let us build for ourselves … a tower whose top will reach into heaven, and let us make for ourselves a name" (Gen. 11:4 NASB). In other words, "Let's construct a monument that puts us in control."

So where did I pick up this notion that I should be in control?

I got it from the garden.

It slipped into my heart in the place where the cosmos first groaned at the primal twisting of God's creation—where not only Adam and Eve but also their children and their children's children began to believe the same lie. The reason I fail to find the glory in my life is that I still want to control the hullabaloo.

Deep inside, so do you.[3]

How to Let Go

How do I release my craving for control? For that matter, if this desire is so deeply rooted in my soul, is it even *possible* for me to let it go? Or, am I destined to spend the rest of my days barely glimpsing the glory of life as it looms on the far side of my delusions of control?

I do think it's possible to replace my craving for control with attitudes that guide me toward a life of glory. After all, even though he was "tempted in all things as we are," Jesus was able to give up his right to be in control. He "emptied himself" and lived in the glory of each present moment (Heb. 4:15; Phil. 2:7 NASB). The question is *how*?

I think I may have run across one possible answer today. I was reading Paul's letter to some Christians in Rome. In this letter, Paul remarks that if people will look around them, they will see that a power more glorious than themselves must have been at work when the cosmos was created: "By taking a long and thoughtful look at what God has created, people have always been able to see what their eyes as such can't see: eternal power, for instance, and the mystery of his divine being" (Rom. 1:20 MSG). In other words, every human being has the capacity to see the glory around us. Yet instead of embracing the glory of God in the hullabaloo of our present lives, we look for glory in the things we can control. Paul describes this process with these words: "They … exchanged the glory of the incorruptible God for an image in the form of corruptible man" (Rom. 1:22–23 NASB).

Drunk on our desire to dominate the direction of our own lives, we turn our backs on authentic glory. In the place of glory we pursue our own fleeting delusions of glory: the home that will satisfy our longing for others' approval, the job that will fulfill our vocational ambitions, the secret steps that will finally lead to lifelong success.

This much you may have picked up already. But what you may not have noticed is what actually causes people to look for glory in things they can control. Here's what, according to Paul, precedes the idolatrous exchange of God's glory for false glories: "They did not … give thanks" (Rom. 1:21).

Did you catch that?

They did not give thanks.

What preceded the idolatrous longing to be in control was a failure to be thankful for the glory that was already available around them.

As I read Paul's words to the Romans, it occurred to me that each time I become frustrated because I can't control my circumstances, the real problem is not my incapacity to manipulate the hullabaloo.

The real problem is that I am not thankful.

I am not thankful for the infinitely glorious gift of this moment of life. Instead of this present moment I want another moment, a different moment with different circumstances. Whenever I fail to be thankful, I am trading my childlike imagination for an image I have molded in the idol factory of my own mind. I exchange the glory of my present life for my own empty visions of glory—visions that lead directly to a realm of anger and frustration.

When this happens, I find myself longing for the supposed glory of some point in the future, craving some moment when everything proceeds according to my plans. I dream about the spring and miss the beauty of winter. I envision houses that I might own in the future and miss the joy of the home God has provided here and now. I fantasize about future vacations, full of blazing sunrises and sandy beaches, and fail to see the simple splendor that surrounds me in this present moment: the cardinal in the evergreen trilling romantic ditties to his sweetheart, the pine tree gently trembling in the breeze, the friends whose lives have fluttered into my path like autumn leaves at precisely the moment I needed them most. Focused on my own fleeting dreams for the future, I become blind to the infinite glory that surrounds me here and now.

The Gift of This Present Moment

So why, after arriving at a lunch appointment twenty minutes late, should I have been thankful? *Because every moment of life—even the twists and turns that I never planned—is a glorious gift from God.*

Did you catch that?

Every moment of life is a glorious gift from God.

Not only the pathways that lead to prosperity and peace.

Not simply the moments that go my way.

Not merely the outcomes that occur according to my plan.

I must learn to be grateful for *every* moment of life because every moment is a gift that is filled with God's own glory. I must be thankful, at the very least, for the fact that I am still experiencing the gift of life. "The sheer wonder of life, of creation, of this place where we find ourselves alive at this moment," Eugene Peterson claims, "requires response, a thank you."[4] Approximately 155,000 people throughout this world slipped into sleep in the past twenty-four hours and never woke up; by God's grace, I was not one of them.[5] Life is a glorious gift, a divine sacrament to be embraced with joy.[6]

Henri Nouwen wrote,

> Gratitude claims this truth that all of life is a pure gift. The discipline of gratitude is the explicit effort to acknowledge that all that I am and all that I have is

> given to me as a gift of love, a gift to be celebrated with joy.... I can choose to be grateful even when my emotions and feelings are still steeped in hurt and resentment.... I can choose to speak about goodness and beauty, even when my inner eye still looks for someone to accuse or something to call ugly.... At many points I have to make a leap of faith to let trust and gratitude have a chance.... And every time I make a little leap, I catch a glimpse of the One who runs out to me and invites me into his joy.[7]

I do not have to be thankful *for* every circumstance, but I am called to be thankful *in* every circumstance (1 Thess. 5:18). Why? Because I possess no gift more glorious than the life that I am living in this present moment. I think Moses was getting at this idea when he sent this request into the heavens: "Teach us to count our days" (Ps. 90:12). "Teach us," in other words, "to know the full value of each present moment."

Practicing the Discipline of Gratitude

So, what if I let go of my idolatrous cravings for control? What if I learned the discipline of gratitude, thanking God for the gift of each moment of existence? What might change in my life's hullabaloo?

A sport-utility vehicle swerves in front of me on the interstate. When I'm groaning beneath the burden of believing that I must be in control, the SUV's sudden presence a few inches from my front bumper threatens my delusions of control, and I become angry. My middle finger remains firmly curled around the steering wheel primarily because this is how some members of my church drive their SUVs and inadvertently flipping the bird at one of them might affect my job security. But when I live in the liberating joy of recognizing that I do not have to be in control, I glimpse glorious possibilities. That's what changes in the midst of my life's hullabaloo. I see that I honestly don't need to be the first person on the exit ramp. I slow down and consider the beauty around me—the blueness of the morning sky, the greenness of the blades of grass, the distant echoes of divine truth rumbling in the form of the raw wailings of John Coltrane's tenor saxophone. In my holier moments, I might even pray for the person in the SUV.

My child skips across the coffee shop and misjudges the distance between her elbow and mine, resulting in my mug of coffee suddenly reduced to steaming espresso and atom-sized ceramic shards. When I am groaning beneath the burden of maintaining control, I see an event I could not control. I mask my embarrassment and fear by erupting in unrestrained rage. In the process I reduce my daughter's joy at spending the day with her daddy into a tearstained specter of self-doubt that whispers, "Why am I so clumsy?"

But when I live in the liberating joy of recognizing every moment as a gift from God, I glimpse greater possibilities. I see that my child is probably sufficiently humiliated at this unexpected eruption of liquid and pottery without me erupting too. I realize that she will learn more from helping the barista clean up the mess than from all the words that I might spew in my anger. And I taste this truth anew: I cannot drink deeply from life's glory until I learn to treat each moment as a gift from God.

I'm late for an appointment. When I groan beneath the

weight of believing I must be in control, I create excuses to pass the blame on to others. I even consider lying about how badly the traffic proceeded around a construction site. In short, I grope desperately in the darkness to regain my idolatrous delusion of control. But when I live in the liberating joy of realizing that this delusion is a barren idol, I become free—free to be honest about my own failures, free to rejoice in each moment of my life, free to be the person that God created me to be.

Your gratitude won't necessarily cause your life's hullabaloo to proceed more smoothly. Even after you begin to release your delusions of control, the gas tank will still become empty, the baby's diaper will still get full, and some months will still outlast the balance in your checking account. And there will still be times when you stink at following Jesus. But, even when you don't receive the gifts you expected, you will remember that you've received a gift greater than your most glorious expectations—the gift of simply being alive. Your gratitude for this gift won't change the unexpected twists in the hullabaloo, but it can keep the unexpected twists from changing you.

Eight

Together: The Trouble with Human Beings

Jesus did not call isolated individuals to follow him. He called a group of disciples. He gathered a crowd.

-William Willimon and Stanley Hauerwas, *Lord, Teach Us*

It is not good that the man should be alone.

-God
Genesis 2:18

During my daughter's first year of dance classes, she performed each month at a care center for the elderly. I don't suppose anyone enjoys visiting nursing homes. I certainly don't. The odors of human waste and antiseptic chemicals seem to struggle with each other in every corridor, and in most cases, the antiseptic scent doesn't seem to be winning.

But it isn't just the odor.

It's the unwelcome recognition that the time may come when I am unable to control my most basic bodily functions. Someday, my tongue may loll uncontrollably. My arms and legs may require restraints because the longings of my mind misjudge the capacities of my flesh.

I do not enjoy visiting nursing homes because there I must touch the awkward truth that I am not immortal. When I look into the furrows time and pain have plowed into these faces, I know I'm seeing a reflection of my own future. And this knowledge is precisely why everyone should visit such places. I need this reminder that my present life will not last forever, and so do you.

It was Hannah's last dance of the year—a Christmas program with big-band tunes from Glenn Miller and Duke Ellington—and the older folks loved it. Near the end as Hannah's troupe tapped a snappy rendition of "Jingle Bells," something happened that no one expected.

One of the residents, a trembling woman clad in a recently soiled lavender sweat suit, stood up and shuffled to the edge of the makeshift dance floor. There, she began to dance. Granted, her trundling movements didn't really qualify as dancing. Her kicks never quite left the ground, her arthritic hands never left her side, and some of her twirls took several moments to complete. Still, the look on her face was one of sheer joy.

What intrigued me were the reactions of the people

around me. Some parents actually seemed annoyed that their children's routine had been interrupted by this woman whose dancing capabilities had peaked in the first half of the previous century. Others smirked at her sagging figure and soiled sweat suit, at this resident so senile that she didn't even know she couldn't dance.

But I didn't see an old woman at all.

What I saw was a young girl—every bit as graceful and full of promise as my girl—twirling in glistening pink tights at her first dance recital so many decades ago. I saw perfect kicks and precise pirouettes. I didn't see a deluded woman in the late winter of her life; I saw a beautiful performer from an era long past.

I suspect that some of the other residents saw that little girl too, because when the music ended, they clapped with all the fervor they could muster. I would have whistled if I could, but I can't, so I just clapped with the residents.

I knew that I had glimpsed something glorious.

And so did everyone else who was able to look beyond the quavering of this woman's body to see the dance that still pulsed in her heart.

I Am Human, and Humans Are Troublesome

As the applause faded, it occurred to me that this is probably how God expects us to look at every person. God longs for us to see glory not only in the rhythms of our own lives, but also in the lives of others. He wants us to see the hidden splendor in every person—a splendor that runs far deeper than their soiled lives and their shuffling struggles to survive. He longs for us to look at them with the boundless imagination of a child, searching past the erratic lurching of their bodies to glimpse the glory that surges in their hearts.

But it's not easy.

It's not easy because human beings are troublesome.

Sure, humans have their moments of beauty and kindness, and they are capable of coming up with some brilliant ideas—democracy, double coupons, Starbucks, and chocolate-covered graham crackers, for instance. But human beings can also be petty, temperamental, self-centered, and lustful. They also require frequent baths.

Because I'm human, I struggle with sin, and sometimes I can be a real jerk. As far as I can tell, I am not alone in this. I suspect you're troublesome too. Simply put, if you or I want to see what's wrong with the human race, the answer is as close as the nearest mirror.

Why God Rejected My Plan

Given these deficiencies in human nature, it seems to me the ideal way for each of us to live a life of glory would be to live alone, separated from other human beings as we seek to see divine splendor in the hullabaloo of our daily lives. If every person pursued this plan, my struggles wouldn't distract you and your troubles wouldn't drag me down.

So far, however, God has not placed his heavenly seal of approval on my plan.

In fact, God has pointed humanity precisely in the opposite direction. The Creator of the universe seems to be convinced that to experience the glory in the hullabaloo, human beings need one another. And this conviction isn't something new; it arose within the fellowship of God before time began.

When he first formed the human race, God created not one but two humans and commanded them to rejoice in the splendor of each other's company (Gen. 1:27–31; 2:18–25). Following the fall and flood, when God conscripted Abraham for divine service, the Creator's deepest desire was for Abraham to father a fellowship of divine glory (Gen. 12:1–3). Still later, when God's glory erupted through a desert shrub and seized the attention of a shepherd named Moses, God's plan was to bind Abraham's offspring together into a faithful community (Ex. 3:7–10). As such, it shouldn't surprise us that when the incarnate God kicked off his earthly ministry, one of his first tasks was to gather a fellowship of followers whose primary purpose was simply "to be with him" (Mark 3:14).

Even after Jesus and these disciples had spent several months crisscrossing Galilee and Judea, Jesus' conviction remained. Remember what he whispered to his Father just a few hours before one of his followers betrayed him?

> I brought glory to you here on earth by doing everything you told me to do.... I am praying not only for these disciples but also for all who will ever believe in me because of their testimony.... I have given them the glory you gave me, so that they may be one, as we are. (John 17:4, 20, 22 NLT)

I pointed out earlier that, according to this text, God has placed his glory in every person who has undertaken the quest to follow Jesus.

This time around, I want you to notice something else about these words. Look at the plural pronouns in this prayer—

them and *these*, *they* and *we*—that Jesus says. Every hint of singularity—*he* or *she*, *him* or *her*—is absent here. Humanity may be troublesome at times, but God is somehow convinced that glory is something that no human can fully experience alone.

Why God Is Never Lonely

Community seems to have been part of what God intended when he placed the first humans in the garden of Eden. "It is not good," the Almighty mused as he surveyed the splendor of his creation, "that the man should be alone" (Gen. 2:18). Somehow, God knew that Adam could not experience the full glory of this planet by himself.

Why do we need one another to experience glory?

Because God is the source of glory, and God is never alone.

At the essence of his being, God is an infinite, intimate fellowship of Father, Son, and Holy Spirit. Long before Jesus burst into space and time, God the Father and God the Son danced with the Spirit,[1] played soccer with the planets, and simply and eternally enjoyed the glorious experience of being God (John 1:1–3). "Let *us* make humankind in *our* image," God announced before human feet ever touched the face of this planet and, in this way, signified that to be created in God's image is to be formed with the purpose of being *together* (Gen. 1:26).

That's what God wants to happen uniquely in the fellowship of his people; he longs for the community that loves him to become a living reflection of his glory. "I have given *them* the glory you gave me," Jesus said to his heavenly Father and thus denoted that the life of glory is practiced in fellowship with others, or it is not practiced at all.

I cannot experience the fullness of this glory until I learn to see glory not only in the rhythms of my own life, but also in the lives of others. I cannot experience glory alone any more than I can get married alone. William Willimon and Stanley Hauerwas said it this way:

> There may be religions that come to you through quiet walks in the woods, or by sitting quietly in the library with a book, or rummaging around in the recesses of your psyche. Christianity is not one of them. Christianity is inherently communal, a matter of life in the Body ... Jesus did not call isolated individuals to follow Him. He called a group of disciples. He gathered a crowd.... Privacy is not a Christian category. We are saved from our privacy by being made part of a people who can tell us what we should do with our money, with our genitals, with our lives. We have been made part of a good company, a wonderful adventure, so that we no longer need "mine."[2]

It is within the hullabaloo of this "good company" that God has hidden his glory. And this glorious assembly doesn't just include folks that are still breathing: "We are," the anonymous writer of Hebrews claims after listing the names of saints long gone, "surrounded by so great a cloud of witnesses" (12:1).

Do you know what that means?

When I gather to worship with the people of God, there is far more glory around me than I may imagine at first glance. The saints of the past—Polycarp of Smyrna and Simon Peter, Martin Luther with his theses and Miriam with her tambourine—swirl and twirl through our fellowship in unseen billows of fire, witnesses to the infinite grandeur of God. They join in the songs that echo around me, and they waltz among the prayers that rise above me.

In a society where many Christians choose a congregation based on which church makes them feel best, it's easy to assume that the presence of divine glory depends on slickly produced worship celebrations and services that meet my needs. And if the church I'm presently attending falls short of my expectations? Captivated by the culture's obsession with more, I can always look for some other congregation that meets more of my desires.

And yet the truth is that whenever God's people gather, there is glory. This glory is present in megachurches and house churches, in ancient hymns and in the latest choruses, in the waters of baptism and in the bread and the cup of Communion. The music may be off-key, the message may last too long, the minister may stumble over some names in the Scripture text, but even in the most ordinary churches there is extraordinary glory. Wherever God's people are together, there is glory. "This is," Rich Mullins once commented, "what liturgy offers that all the razzmatazz of our modern worship can't touch.... You go home from church going, 'Wow, I just took communion and you know what? If Augustine were alive today, he would have had it with me and maybe he is and maybe he did.'"[3]

Getting Out of My "Solitary Conceit"

And why has God gone to such great lengths to infuse the fellowship of his people with glory? What does God want out of all this?

Simply this: God's desire is for glory to be so obvious in his people that the entire world stands in awe (see Isa. 43:4–7). What God wants is for the world to look at his church and see a people who find glory, not in constantly accumulating more, but in the ordinary splendor of the journey we share. And how do we accomplish God's plan? It happens as God's people learn to see glory in one another. That's why Jesus told his Father, "The glory that you have given me I have given them, so that they may be one, as we are one … so that the world may know that you have sent me" (John 17:22–23).

When I look at the people in my church, I do frequently glimpse glory. I contemplate the crazy collection of fellow travelers that surrounds me on Sundays, and I see a glorious mosaic of grace—young and old, rich and poor, brown and black and white—all drawn to this place by the grace of God. In these moments I stand amazed at this tangible evidence of divine glory around me.

Most of the time.

But as I said before, human beings are troublesome. And for some reason, God does not choose to change this aspect of our natures immediately when we enter into a relationship with Jesus. I do not know why God works this way; perhaps it's simply because he isn't in a hurry. I suppose he can afford to take his time. After all, he has not only all the time in the world but also all the time in the next world.

What's frustrating about this sort of patience is that, because God is willing to work so slowly, some people still act like jerks for several decades after they embrace God's grace. Someone once commented that the church is a lot like Noah's ark—if it weren't for the storm on the outside, no one could stand the fact that it smells like you-know-what on the inside. In the simplest possible terms, some of the people whom God calls to himself don't seem very glorious.

Like people whose political preferences don't mesh with mine.

Like people who complain about every change in the church.

Like people who interrupt my schedule to talk for hours about absolutely nothing.

Like people who leave the church instead of sticking it out and learning to see glory in the people around them.

Like people whose personal beliefs are a little quirky, who wouldn't be so bad if only they could keep quiet about their pet theory that the Antichrist will arise from the U.S. Postal Service and that those computerized markings on each envelope are actually the mark of the beast.

Like ... well, like all the people who aren't like me. Come to think of it, if everyone could be just like me, the church would be a much more glorious place.

Or so I believe in those moments when I give in to the serpent's soft-pedaled lie—the lie that suggests to my soul that the life of glory revolves around people like me.

But the people whom God has placed in my church aren't like me, and that's precisely the point. They aren't supposed to be. Part of the scandal of the cross of Christ is that the persons who rub shoulders in the shadow of his cross are people that the world would never dream of mingling together (1 Cor. 1:18, 23–29; Gal. 3:28). Put another way, I cannot truly love God until I love my neighbor. And according to Jesus, I don't have the privilege of picking my neighbors. In fact, my neighborhood is as large as God's love, or at least it's supposed to be (see Luke 10:25–37).

In the absence of fellowship with others, it's easy to convince myself that the glory of life revolves around me. But the glory of life is too vast and multihued to be limited to my personal experiences. I desperately need fellow travelers on my pilgrimage to find the kingdom of God in the hullabaloo of my daily life. They are my reminders that the life of glory is not about me. Perhaps C. S. Lewis said it best when he reminisced about his early years as a believer:

> When I first became a Christian, about fourteen years ago, I thought that I could do it on my own, by retiring to my rooms and reading theology, and I wouldn't go to the churches and Gospel Halls; … I disliked very much their hymns, which I considered to be fifth-rate poems set to sixth-rate music. But as I went on I saw the great merit of it. I came up against different people of quite different outlooks and different education, and then gradually my conceit just began peeling off. I realized that the hymns (which were just sixth-rate music) were, nevertheless, being sung with devotion and benefit by an old saint in elastic-side boots in the opposite pew, and then you realize that you aren't fit to clean those boots. It gets you out of your solitary conceit.[4]

Imagining Glory

And all of this sounds great until you go to a church and discover that you don't quite fit the social profile this congregation expects. Or the preacher entangles the profound beauty of God's Word with propaganda from a particular political party. Or you recognize there are church members and even church leaders who are willing to manipulate people's feelings for personal profit.

This doesn't seem very glorious—and it isn't.

I can't defend everything people have done in the name of

Jesus. Much of it has no defense; it's simply *wrong*. I do know this, though. In every place where Jesus is recognized as Savior and God, there *is* glory. It may not reside in the most prominent people or in the most vocal ones, but the glory is there.

How do you find it?

It takes looking beyond fellow believers' faltering attempts to follow the rhythms of God and seeing the divine dance that pulses in their hearts.

It takes a childlike imagination.

I think that's the point of Jesus' parable about the final judgment. The King of the Universe separates his creatures, sending the sheep to his right and the goats to his left. Then, he speaks to those on his right:

> "Enter, you who are blessed by my Father!… I was hungry and you fed me, I was thirsty and you gave me a drink, I was homeless and you gave me a room, I was shivering and you gave me clothes, I was sick and you stopped to visit, I was in prison and you came to me.… I tell you the truth, whatever you did for one of the least of these brothers of mine, you did for me." Then he will say to those on his left, "Depart from me, you who are cursed, into the eternal fire prepared for the devil and his angels. For I was hungry and you gave me nothing to eat, I was thirsty and you gave me nothing to drink, I was a stranger and you did not invite me in, I needed clothes and you did not clothe me, I was sick and in prison and you did not look after me.… I tell you the truth, whatever you did not do for one of the least of these, you did not do for me." (Matt. 25:34–36 MSG; Matt. 25:40–43, 45 NIV)

Those who entered into the Father's kingdom were able to look at "the least of these"—at the people with the deepest needs—and imagine glory.

What if you did this? What if you decided to root your life in a certain community of faith instead of skipping from church to church, always searching for a place to meet your expectations—one more indication of our culture's persistent lust for more? And what if you decided that you *would* imagine glory among these people that surround you?

What about the child whose hygienic habits leave much to be desired? Seen through the eyes of Jesus, perhaps she's a future missionary searching for someone willing to listen to her dreams.

What about the church member who lacks certain social skills—you know, the one who always wants to talk precisely when you need to leave? What if he's a messenger from the throne of God, an angel of highest heaven in a tattered sweatshirt and threadbare shoes (Heb. 13:2)?

And what about all the people from whom you'd prefer to turn away—"the poor, the crippled, the blind, and the lame" (Luke 14:21)? What if you viewed them all as signposts of God's kingdom, echoes of infinite glory shrouded in veils of human flesh?

What if you imagined glory in each one?

Someone else imagined this sort of glory, you know.

Once upon a time there was a Jewish carpenter who had a habit of seeing more in others than they could see in themselves. He was abandoned and betrayed by people who had promised to follow him to the end. Still, he imagined glory, not only in the people who loved him, but also in those who didn't. He looked into the eyes of his betrayer and whispered, "Friend" (Matt. 26:50). He stared at the soldiers whose spit still mingled with the blood and tears in his ragged beard and said, "Father, forgive them" (Luke 23:34). He embraced the disciple who had denied him and whispered, "Feed my lambs" (John 21:15). And to this day, he looks at the likes of you and me and says, "You are the light of the world" (Matt. 5:14).

Now that takes some imagination.

Movement Three
Glory Where You Never Expected It

Lord, I have a great idea:
Be more selective about where
you expect me to see
your glory.
I'm having a tough time seeing anything glorious
    in hotheaded church members,
    in hygienically challenged children,
    in the excessively amorous homosexual couple
    sitting two booths away from me
    in a downtown restaurant.
Just for a moment, Lord,
could you let me be
a bit more selective
about these possibilities?
I prefer to see glory in people
    who are laid-back,
    well-groomed, and whose
    orientations match mine.
But if I claim to be
    part of your story,
I can't be selective
    about these possibilities.
After all,
    you weren't selective
    when you glanced
        in my direction.
If you had been,
    you would have never
    placed your glory
    in me.

Nine

Interruptions: Why Bad Karma Isn't Necessarily a Bad Thing

"Rabbi, who sinned, this man or his parents, that he was born blind?"

—A follower of Jesus, John 9:2

God made everything beautiful in itself and in its time—but he's left us in the dark, so we can never know what God is up to, whether he's coming or going.

—Ecclesiastes 3:11 MSG

A treasure lay across the palms of my hands. When I first spotted it, it had glistened like an onyx stream nearly hidden amid the grass and honeysuckle that edged the playground. Its delicate body—glossy black and nearly a yard long—was wrinkled into a series of small kinks, and a cream-colored swath ran along its belly. In this simple treasure my childlike imagination glimpsed vast, untapped possibilities.

What lay across my trembling hands was a snake.

A black rat snake, to be exact.

Not a live one, mind you. This one was mostly headless and appeared to have been an unwitting victim of the swirling blades of the school's lawnmower. Still, seen through the eyes of an eight-year-old boy, it was a treasure.

I was an unselfish child, so as my eyes caressed the deceased creature's intricate sequence of scales, I made a momentous decision. I would not keep my treasure to myself. The joy of this treasure was simply too great not to share.

I scanned the playground of the small Christian school, searching for someone who might appreciate this treasure. The afternoon kickball game seemed to have absorbed everyone else's attention. Girls scampered around the bases as their knee-length navy jumpers snapped in the wind. One of the boys, clad in a patriotic necktie and corduroy pants that sang a rapid *zhwip-zhwip* as he ran, was pursuing a red-haired fourth-grader, faded kickball clutched beneath his arm.

Technically, I was playing kickball too. During the first few weeks of the school year, my teacher, Mrs. Redwing, informed me that I had to play kickball every day so that I could learn teamwork and school spirit. But right now I was in the distant outfield, and I had forgotten which team I was on … again.

Which team I was on didn't really matter anyway

because my involvement had never affected a game's outcome, except for the one time when I wandered into the path of an oncoming ball and accidentally caught it. My good fortune excited everyone until another student pointed out that I wasn't supposed to be in the outfield in the first place because my team was kicking. I had somehow missed the transition between the innings. That moment represented the peak of my kickball career.

After my career peaked that fall, a new position was created to match my distinctive skills: I frequently played on both teams as the permanent outfielder. When I served as the permanent outfielder, the team captains placed me *way* outfield, several yards past the point where any normal elementary student might land a ball. As a result I learned teamwork and school spirit by wandering through the tall grass and trees along the edge of the playground. Ironically, this was how I had wanted to learn teamwork and school spirit in the first place, so now everyone was happy.

Today I was learning the ways of the Force with Luke Skywalker and Jedi Master Yoda. I had located Darth Vader in a dark crevice between the knotted roots of a walnut tree. I had nearly defeated Vader in an epic lightsaber battle that lasted most of recess, but when I glimpsed the snake, I decided to let Vader go. Now it was time to share my joy. The problem was, everyone else was too focused on the kickball game to appreciate my treasure.

Everyone except Rachel.

Rachel was one of my fellow fourth-graders; she had mouse-brown hair, and she spent recesses in the sandbox beside the swing sets. I think this was because she lacked the requisite skills to achieve the coveted position of permanent outfielder. Or maybe it was because she had somehow gained an exemption from learning teamwork and school spirit. Either way, Rachel's back was turned to me, and she was building something in the sand.

Girls! I snorted when I glimpsed her elaborate sand castle. *Never able to live in the real world.*

I slipped quietly behind her, still contemplating how I could best share my joy. At this point I should mention that nowhere in the school's detailed rule book had anyone mentioned what students were allowed to do with decapitated snakes. The school's rules described in detail how true Christians tapered their hair, avoided rock music and dancing, and always pushed in their chairs—presumably because tapered haircuts, beatless music, and well-arranged chairs were such vital parts of Jesus' earthly ministry. But *nowhere* did the school rules say anything about what students could do with headless rat snakes. I knew this because I had reviewed the rule book that morning while the chapel speaker was preaching about being attentive to the Scriptures.

By the time I reached the sandbox, my decision was made. I stretched out my hand and shared my joy.

The snake vanished down the back of Rachel's jumper.

And Rachel began to rejoice, squealing in ecstasy and leaping around the sandbox. Clearly, she didn't realize that dancing was against the school's rules. I kindly pointed out that she could be expelled for this brazen breach of the school's standards, but Rachel was in no mood to listen. She continued to prance around the sandbox like the lead singer on Van Halen's video for the song "Runnin' with the Devil." (I had watched this video once and listened to the music because, according to the school's rules, this was the Devil's music, and I wanted to make certain I knew what it sounded like. That way, if anyone brought such music to school, I could report it to the principal. In addition to being an unselfish child, I was also very concerned with maintaining my school's high moral standards.)

Unable to deter Rachel from the dark path to destruction that begins with dancing, I shook the sand from my feet and returned to the distant outfield. At the edge of the playground I resumed the crucial position of permanent outfielder, hoping that I hadn't missed anything important—such as the return of Darth Vader.

Here I was, learning teamwork and school spirit when Mrs. Redwing burst through the tall grass, towing Rachel behind her. Rachel's eyes were red-rimmed, almost as if she had been crying.

I knew it, I thought. *Busted for dancing.*

At this point it became clear that Mrs. Redwing did not share my perspective on the rat snake's inestimable value. Even though her fist was clenched tightly around my treasure, her face was far from joyful. In fact, she seemed downright angry. (Angry outbursts were, by the way, also forbidden in the school's rule book.)

I don't recall what Mrs. Redwing said on the way to the building, primarily because I was concerned about whether a teacher could be suspended for breaking the school's rule against angry outbursts. When we arrived at the principal's office, it became clear that something had gone horribly wrong.

I was the one in trouble.

This was quite frustrating, if you want to know the truth.

Rachel had danced like David Lee Roth.

Mrs. Redwing had engaged in an angry outburst.

I had spent most of recess learning teamwork and school spirit in the distant outfield. Yet, somehow, *I* was the one in trouble. At this point in my life I had never heard of karma or reincarnation, and I still don't buy into either concept. However, if I had believed in such fantasies, I would have wondered what dastardly deed I had commitment in a previous life to deserve such injustice.

Then, it got worse: They made me tell Rachel that I was sorry. I was *not* sorry, but they made me say it anyway. This was a lie, and lying was against the school's rules too. Worst of all, Mrs. Redwing kept my snake. My teacher stole from me. This also was prohibited in the rule book. When I helpfully pointed out that Mrs. Redwing could be expelled for stealing my snake, the principal succumbed to an angry outburst—yet another violation of the school's rules—that resulted in me remaining after school for several days.

I was supposed to survey the book of Proverbs during my detention, which I assumed would tell me what I should do with headless snakes in the future. After several chapters the author of Proverbs still hadn't addressed my circumstances nearly as clearly as I had hoped. King Solomon seemed more concerned with making wise choices, whatever that meant.

I had kept every rule in the school's manual and still, somehow, left the principal's office with a detention slip in my hand. I realized that keeping the rules and planning well does not guarantee everything in my life will turn out the way I intend. I suppose that's what Robert Burns meant when he penned the familiar lines, "The best laid schemes o' mice and men/Gang aft a-gley;/And leave us naught but grief and pain/For promised joy."[1] Or maybe Mr. Burns just had an unnatural fixation on rodents.

In any case, a crucial truth occurred to me in the principal's office: *There's a glitch in the hullabaloo.* Or at least it feels that way. I wouldn't have put it that way at the time, of course. Then I simply would have whined, "It's not fair!" But the basic idea remains the same.

For awhile it's possible to live with the assumption that whenever unwanted interruptions shatter my dreams, there must have been something I did wrong, and sometimes this assumption is correct. There are times when unwelcome interruptions disturb the flow of my life because I could have made better choices.[2] Truth be told, life works this way so often that it's easy to assume life *always* operates this way. In this line of thinking, what I put into life determines what I get out of it. The Eastern religions have lashed this principle to the wheel of *samsara* and dubbed it "karma," but it isn't only Hindus and Buddhists who assume life operates in tidy cause-and-effect sequences. So do I, whenever my soul groans, "What did I do to deserve *this?"*

You'd think that as long as we plan well and keep all the rules, the hullabaloo should always proceed smoothly, sweeping our lives upward to places of prosperity and peace. But it doesn't work that way. Despite my finest intentions, an unanticipated beat or two always seems to disrupt the rhythms of my life at precisely the moments I least expect it. Put another way, I can keep all the rules, possess the best of intentions, and still end up in the principal's office.

Why I Don't Have My Own Television Program

You've been there too, haven't you? No, not in the principal's office trying to get your snake back. But I bet there have been times when you have thought, "If I plan well and possess all the best intentions, everything should turn out fine." But then, things haven't turned out fine, and you've found yourself wondering, *Where is the glory in this?*

Most of life's interruptions are mere ripples on the surface of the hullabaloo, minor inconveniences that will be forgotten in a month or two. There's the unexpected lurch of the table that lands a chock-full espresso latte squarely in the middle of your notebook computer, the road construction that turns your perfectly planned morning into a livid rush to avoid an unfashionably late arrival at work, the trivial project that somehow morphs into a massive headache, the undeserved trip to the principal's office. Each event seems so small once you finally consign it to your book of memories. Yet it's the frustration you feel in the midst of each one that bleeds the glory from your daily life.

There are other interruptions too—ones that can't be so easily consigned to a forgotten shelf in the library of your life. These are the interruptions that leave you facedown in the shambles of your shattered dreams, wondering what went wrong.

You already know the sort of interruptions I'm talking about, don't you? Maybe you've even lived through one or two of them.

You tried everything to keep the marriage together, but your spouse still says, "It's over."

You ate right and exercised, but your physician still says, "It's hopeless."

You did your best to manage your business well, but the accountant still says, "It's bankrupt."

You worked your hardest and kept the rules, but the pink slip still makes it clear: "It's time for another job."

How do you learn to look at these interruptions with childlike imagination?

What makes these circumstances even more frustrating is that some popular religious personalities support the idea that if you follow God's will, God somehow guarantees that you'll spend your days in prosperity and peace. I occasionally flip through a few religious stations and watch one or two preachers until my desire to hurl the remote control through the television screen becomes dangerously strong. This means I typically watch between twenty and thirty seconds of each program before I change the channel.

In these brief forays into religious broadcasting, I've discovered that Hurricane Katrina never would have made landfall if the United States government would have allowed homosexuals to be stoned to death, that the bird flu will soon decimate North America because millions of people watched *The Da Vinci Code* movie, and that unless I spend fifty-five dollars on a six-dollar cubic-zirconia "Jesus" pendant, millions of devoted viewers will be deprived of hearing these cause-and-effect connections between tragedy and iniquity. In every case the unspoken assumption seems to be that whenever unwelcome interruptions shatter people's lives, it's because someone didn't follow the right rules.

It isn't only on television that I've glimpsed this theological perspective. I've watched the faith of an entire family wither under the relentless heaviness of this worldview. I've seen it at the funeral of a three-month-old baby, where I gripped a grandmother's shoulder as she screamed, "What did I do wrong?" I've seen it in the intensive care unit, where a mother, recently free from years of drug addiction, whispered as her daughter fought for life in the aftermath of an automobile accident, "I did what God wanted. I got my life straightened out. If God doesn't come through and heal my daughter now, I don't know what I'll do." And still this perspective seems to persist in many of the most popular Christian books and television programs.

I don't buy into this worldview, which may explain why I don't have my own television program. But I feel sorry for the well-meaning people who buy into this cause-and-effect understanding of God. I even feel sorry for the television preachers, who probably aren't trying to tell such ridiculous lies. *How miserable it must be,* I have come to realize, *to live believing that whenever tragedy strikes, it's because you've done something sinful*. Truth be told, I know exactly how miserable this feels because, once upon a time, I believed it too. It's what tore so deeply into my soul in the months that I waited for the child to call my own. I thought if I did everything that God wanted, he would give me the desire of my heart. But then God didn't give me my heart's desire, and it seemed to me I had been betrayed by the one who loves me most. Karma may make logical sense, but it doesn't work in real life.

Still, there's a part of me that sometimes wants the hullabaloo to work like karma—a predictable cause-and-effect sequence through which sinners see their lives shattered by unwelcome interruptions while prudent people watch their plans flourish and prosper. This longing is what drives the idolatrous notion that if we could only locate the right series of steps to success, the deepest longings of our souls will be forever satisfied. It's what draws us away from the glory in the hullabaloo toward a frenzied scramble for more.

Living in the Land of "If Only"

Here's the central problem with living as if what I put into life determines what I get out of it: When unwelcome interruptions burst into my life, I find my soul moving to a realm I call "the Land of If Only." Whenever I reside in the Land of If Only, I spend my days goading myself with guilt, constantly resolving to plan better next time: *If only* I had made some different choices, my life would have turned out glorious and happy. *If only* I had paid closer attention, this tragedy never would have happened. *If only* I had worked a little harder, I wouldn't be stuck in this dead-end job. When I live in the Land of If Only, I do not see the glory in the hullabaloo; I see only my own failures, which I believe have caused my life not to turn out right.

I'm not the first person who has spent time in the Land of If Only. This was, in fact, the homeland of some of Jerusalem's most prominent religious thinkers during the years of Jesus' ministry.[3] As I write these words I imagine the rabbi from Nazareth slipping into the temple courts on a spring afternoon. A blind man begs for a few copper coins in the shadow of a gate gilded in gold. The rabbi's students toss a sideward glance into the beggar's unseeing eyes. Their souls surge with the same pangs you might feel as you bypass the homeless man begging beside the exit ramp—a recognition of responsibility for this reflection of God's image coupled with a desperate desire to distance yourself from the beggar. After a few awkward glances in other directions, the disciples try to drown their pangs in the river of their own self-righteousness: "Rabbi," one of them whispers, "who sinned, this man or his parents, that he was born blind?" (John 9:2). Put another way, "If only everyone would have done everything right, blindness wouldn't have interrupted this man's life. So, who messed up?"

The disciples were living in the Land of If Only.[4]

I still live there too sometimes.

I too have caught myself looking at another person's tragedy, wondering what they did to deserve it. I too have stood in the shadow of my own life's interruptions and felt my chest clench beneath the weight of my whispered wish, "If only I would have …" I too have blamed myself for interruptions that were beyond my control, and it works for a while.

But then it happens.

At some point I'm struck with an interruption that "if only" cannot explain.

An interruption that jolts my delusion that life works according to tidy cause-and-effect sequences.

A recognition that, though I am in control of my choices, I am not in control of my life.

A point at which I whisper, "If only I would have ... " and then realize there was nothing else I could have done.

In these moments I am forced to come to terms with this painful truth: There are no surefire steps for me to follow that will somehow guarantee a life filled with glory if only I keep each step closely enough. Simply because unwelcome interruptions shatter my life doesn't mean I've sinned, and doing what's right doesn't guarantee my life will always be pleasant or prosperous.

Jesus knew this truth when he turned from his puzzled students and smiled gently at the blind man whose mind never could have conceived the miracle that was about to overtake him. "It was neither that this man sinned, nor his parents," Jesus chuckled as he began to brush some dust into his palm, "but it was so that the works of God might be displayed in him" (John 9:3 NASB). Then Jesus healed him.

And this story sounds great, unless, of course, you're the blind man who ended up rejected by the religious leaders because Jesus healed him (John 9:34). This man, even after being healed, may not have possessed any marketable skills, because he had spent the best years of his life begging.

I know this doesn't sound terribly spiritual, but let's be honest: Jesus still didn't do much to balance the ledger of cosmic justice in this man's favor. In fact, when you take an honest look at the Gospels, Jesus seems notoriously unconcerned with balancing ledgers in favor of his followers.

Jesus drops everything to run to a total stranger's house to heal his servant, but he dawdles four days when his friend Lazarus writhes in the jaws of death (see John 11:1–6). On his way to heal the daughter of a respectable religious leader, the Messiah strolls off-course to assist a social outcast who randomly seizes the fringe of his cloak. Meanwhile, the religious leader waits helplessly as his only daughter suffers, and before it's over Jesus allows the little girl to *die* (Mark 5:21–35). When John the Baptist—the one Jesus dubbed the "greatest" of the prophets—languishes on death row, Jesus doesn't show up at all, not even for a weekend visit as far as we know (Matt. 11:1–11).[5]

With stories like these forming its foundation, it's a wonder Christianity has gained so many devotees over the centuries. And that's not even taking into account what has happened since Jesus' ascension—the deaths of Stephen and James, Paul's "thorn in the flesh," the elder John's exile on Patmos, my trip to the principal's office, and the unexpected tragedies that force you to see what you put into life isn't necessarily what you get out of it (Acts 7:59; 12:2; 2 Cor. 12:7; Rev. 1:9). Something seems desperately wrong with this picture.

The Problem with God and Karma

If God's primary purpose is to keep the cosmic karma balanced, someone needs to reevaluate the Almighty's managerial effectiveness. Sure, God has promised to balance everything at the end of time, but amid the hubbub and hullabaloo of people's present lives, God doesn't seem particularly proficient at balancing ledgers in favor of the righteous.

This is a problem, it seems to me.

Unless, of course, manipulating the hullabaloo to prosper righteous people isn't at the top of God's to-do list. Unless God's deepest desires have nothing to do with balance or karma or cosmic ledgers. Unless, perhaps, what God wants most is to fill every portion of the hullabaloo—even the interruptions—with glory. If so, perhaps the problem isn't with God's management but with our expectations.

The truth is that I cannot control the hullabaloo, and I wasn't intended to. Hullabaloo is messy, unpredictable, and far too complex to fit into my finite formulas. It is, to borrow a phrase from the book of Ecclesiastes, as elusive as "the path of the wind" and as mysterious as the weaving of "bones ... in the womb of the pregnant woman" (Eccl. 11:5 NASB).

I do not say the hullabaloo is beyond God's control—it isn't. But the hullabaloo is beyond my capacity to control its outcome or to predict its eddies. All the "if only's" that frame my responses to the dark side of the hullabaloo are merely my own foolish attempts to maintain the delusion that I can cause the hullabaloo to turn out the way I expect. As I discovered on a spring afternoon more than two decades ago, I can keep all the rules, make the best of plans, and still end up in the principal's office.

Oh, and Rachel, if you ever happen to read this book, I'm sorry if I hurt your feelings. I really am. But I'm still not sorry for dropping the snake down your jumper.

That moment was—for lack of a better term—absolutely *glorious*.

Ten

Unfairness: Living as Though the Glory Goes On

LIFE ISN'T FAIR; IT'S JUST FAIRER THAN DEATH, THAT'S ALL.

—THE PRINCESS BRIDE

THOUGH I DO MY WORK WITH WISDOM, KNOWLEDGE, AND SKILL, I MUST LEAVE EVERYTHING I GAIN TO PEOPLE WHO HAVEN'T WORKED TO EARN IT. THIS IS NOT ONLY FOOLISH BUT HIGHLY UNFAIR.

—ECCLESIASTES 2:21 NLT

You may conclude that I'm crazy—if you do, you probably won't be alone—but I happen to believe that the glory of life is present in its fullness in every part of the hullabaloo, even in the interruptions.

But there's a catch—a difficult admission I must make before I can see glory in the interruptions.

What's the catch?

Simply this: I cannot begin to glimpse the glory in the interruptions until I release the absurd expectation that God is somehow responsible for causing all of my plans to prosper. Before I can live in glory, I must vacate the Land of If Only. Sentences such as "It's not fair" and "What did I do to deserve this?" must vanish from my vocabulary. After all, as Edith declares in *The Princess Bride:*

> "Life isn't fair, Bill. We tell our children that it is, but it's a terrible thing to do. It's not only a lie, it's a cruel lie. Life isn't fair." …
>
> "It isn't!" I said, so loud I really startled her. "You're right! It's not fair." I was so happy if I'd known how to dance, I'd have started dancing.… "Life isn't fair; it's just fairer than death, that's all."[1]

The author of Ecclesiastes was just as blunt about this truth, though he wasn't quite so excited about it:

> Though I do my work with wisdom, knowledge, and skill, I must leave everything I gain to people who haven't worked to earn it. This is not only foolish but

> highly unfair.... God gives great wealth and honor to some people and gives them everything they could ever want, but then he doesn't give them the health to enjoy it. They die, and others get it all! This is meaningless—a sickening tragedy. (Eccl. 2:21; 6:2 NLT)

I live in a world where, according to some scientists, the mere flip of a butterfly's wing can eventually spawn a tornado—a world in which God has granted a measure of freedom not only to women and men but also to wind and waves, sparrows and snails.[2] In such a world, there is no guarantee of fairness. The central image of Christian faith is not, after all, a set of well-balanced scales; it is an execution stake on which a righteous man was tortured to death. If fairness had been a fundamental guarantee of human existence, I would have been the one on the cross.

Glory in the Interruptions

God is not in the business of balancing the hullabaloo in favor of the righteous; he is in the business of *glory*. And this glory has nothing to do with whether or not my life proceeds according to my plans. It has everything to do with whether or not I will embrace the glory that is present in my life, even when my most precious plans fall through.

Please don't miss my point: I am not telling you that God directly causes every interruption in your life. What's more, I'm not proclaiming the sadistic notion that you must somehow enjoy tragedy. What I'm trying to point out is that God has never committed himself to balance tragic interruptions with more fortunate ones. What he has chosen to do is something far greater than manipulating the hullabaloo in your favor. Remember Paul's proclamation on Mars Hill? "In him we live and move and exist," the apostle claimed (Acts 17:28 NLT). Paul's phrase "in him" apparently includes every part of life, even your least-welcome interruptions. Every moment of life—even the smallest interruption—is, in the words of C. S. Lewis, "big with God … and every bush (could we but perceive it) a Burning Bush."[3] The Lord of Glory has poured his own presence into the hullabaloo. And, because God has lavished the gift of glory in the ordinary rhythms of your life, every instant of your life already teems with the possibility of glory.

Let's face it, though: Even after we've released the notion that God is responsible to balance the hullabaloo in our favor, there are still times when it's difficult to see glory in the interruptions.

So, how do you do it? How can you glimpse glory in the day-to-day interruptions that pierce your life? How do you taste glory divine when unwelcome circumstances turn your life into chaos?

Glory Goes On

Truth be told, I'm still struggling to do this. My mind knows that all the segments of my life—even the interruptions—are swollen to the point of bursting with glory divine. But my heart, well, that's another matter. More often than I care to admit, my heart still doesn't get it.

However, I have grasped at least one truth that helps. I found it when I read the book of Job. The truth is simply this: *Learn to live as if the glory goes on.*

According to the opening verses of the book bearing his name, Job kept every rule and possessed the best intentions. He was "blameless, upright, fearing God and turning away from evil" (Job 1:1 NASB). He was a paragon of moral virtue—much like me when I slipped the snake down the back of Rachel's jumper.

What's more, Job was ridiculously rich; his file cabinets overflowed with registration papers for more than ten thousand animals. Not surprisingly, his plans for his future were full of glory: "I thought, 'I'll die peacefully in my own bed, grateful for a long and full life, a life deep-rooted and well-watered, a life limber and dew-fresh, my soul suffused with glory'" (Job 29:18–20 MSG).

But that was before the band of marauders massacred his servants and stole his donkeys and oxen.

And before the unexpected flash of lightning sparked a wildfire that destroyed all of his sheep and shepherds.

Before the Chaldeans drove his camels into the western wastelands.

Before a cyclone tore into the house of his firstborn son and took the lives of Job's ten children.

Before the boils began to blossom on the surface of his skin.

Before he was reduced to a mere fragment of a man, his flesh encrusted with boils from the crown of his head to the soles of his feet.

Before his pain became so great that he screamed into the sky, "Obliterate the day I was born. Blank out the night I was conceived! … Why didn't I die at birth, my first breath out of the womb my last?" (Job 3:3, 11 MSG).

Despite Job's repeated requests, no reply tumbled from the heavens—no apologies, no encouragement, and no explanation for the unwelcome interruptions that were grinding his righteous life into the dirt.

Before it was over, every remnant of glory had been torn from Job's life: "He has stripped from me my glory," Job groaned, "and taken the crown from my head" (Job 19:9 ESV). And still, heaven remained silent.

Job's closest friends seem to have served as the self-help gurus of the land of Uz. Their cause-and-effect theology foreshadowed many of the current messages of religious television: If you follow God's rules and plan well, you'll always have wealth and wisdom to spare. *If Job is experiencing this much tragedy,* Job's friends reasoned, *he must have done something wrong. If only he will recognize his failures, everything will be okay.* Job's friends were permanent citizens of the Land of If Only.

"Think!" Eliphaz the Temanite demanded of Job. "Has a truly innocent person ever ended up on the scrap heap? ... It's my observation that those who plow evil and sow trouble reap evil and trouble" (Job 4:7–8 MSG). "Here's what you must do," Bildad echoed. "Get down on your knees before God Almighty. If you're as innocent and upright as you say, it's not too late" (Job 8:5–6 MSG).

But Job sticks to his guns; these tragic interruptions couldn't have resulted from any hidden sin. He's confessed every sin he's committed, and he's made the most righteous plans. "Even if [the Lord] killed me, I'd keep on hoping," Job claims. "I'd defend my innocence to the very end.... Can anyone prove charges against me?" (Job 13:15, 19 MSG).

This argument lasts for thirty-four chapters, and no one backs down. Job keeps crying for an answer, the heavens remain silent as stone, and Job's friends keep reminding him that his repentance must precede God's reply.

Then comes the wind.

At first, it breathes gently across the plains of Uz, the unseen sighing of a planet still longing for redemption. Then, the sigh begins to swirl and twirl and gather potency until Job and his friends can hardly hear one another's eloquent speeches. When one of Job's companions pauses his lecture long enough to grab a single gasping breath, speech erupts from the whirlwind. It seems as if the cosmos has been contemplating these words for millennia and only now has found a mouthpiece sufficiently wondrous and wild to shake the earth with its wisdom.

But this is not the voice of creation.

This is the voice of the Creator, bellowing from the whirlwind.

God doesn't explain; God explodes.

And God doesn't offer his servant a single reason why his life hasn't proceeded according to tidy cause-and-effect sequences. (As it turns out, it was a supracelestial deal between God and the Devil—but no one lets Job in on this secret.) Instead, God hurls questions at Job, and they aren't questions about the problems of pain, evil, and suffering in the world either. No, the questions on this quiz are mostly about astronomy, zoology, meteorology, and macrobiology.

> Brace yourself, because I have some questions for you, and you must answer them.... Who defined the boundaries of the sea as it burst from the womb, and as I clothed it with clouds and thick darkness? ... Can you hold back the movements of the stars? ... Can you shout to the clouds and make it rain? ... Have you watched as the wild deer are born? Do you know how many months they carry their young? Are you aware of the time of their delivery? ... Do you still want to argue with the Almighty? You are God's critic, but do you have the answers? (Job 38:3, 8–9, 31, 34; 39:1–2; 40:2 NLT)

God doesn't answer a single question Job has asked. And somehow Job is satisfied with that response: "I know that you can do anything, and no one can stop you," he whispers into the divine whirlwind, cloak clutched around his boil-scarred face. "You ask, 'Who is this that questions my wisdom with such ignorance?' It is I. And I was talking about things I did not understand, things far too wonderful for me" (Job 42:2–3 NLT).

Why Was Job Satisfied?

After reading this exchange I'm left wondering, *How could this encounter possibly have satisfied Job?* Job is encrusted in scabs and tears, facedown in a heap of ashes, and God forces him to endure a midterm examination about wild deer, coastal flood plains, and Middle Eastern weather patterns. And, somehow, this *satisfies* Job.

Why?

It's true, as others have pointed out, that what Job needed most wasn't an *answer* but an *assurance*—an assurance that God had not forgotten him. Still, I'm left with the question, *What's the point of this litany of questions about God's creation? Why the queries about seas and stars and the mating habits of mammals? How can these questions satisfy the longings of Job's soul?*

At first it seems like God is being a celestial smart aleck, proudly flaunting his omnipotence in the face of Job's pain. But a few weeks ago I glimpsed something in these chapters that I'd never recognized before.

Job has thrown this accusation into his Creator's face: "[The Lord] has stripped from me my glory and taken the crown from my head" (Job 19:9 ESV). In other words, "I may have been created to live in glory, but the glory of my life is gone; God himself has taken it away." When God unleashes his litany of questions, he is hinting at a crucial truth about the life of glory.

What is this truth?

Simply this: *The glory goes on.*

Each query that God hurls in Job's direction points to some reflection of divine glory in the hullabaloo of daily living—a stretch of shoreline that somehow suppresses an ocean stretching far beyond the limits of human sight, the crisscrossing sweep of the planets across a star-strewn sky, the soaring of hawk and eagle along a distant horizon, the delicate wonder of a newborn fawn (Job 38:4–11, 31–33; 39:1–3, 26–30).

Even when interruptions shattered Job's life, each signpost of divine glory continued: The oceans kept pressing against shores of sand and stone, the stars never ceased to shine, birds of prey still soared sapphire skies, the wild animals continued to care for their young. Even though Job felt as though his tragedies had stripped away every remnant of glory, it still pulsed all around him, hidden beneath a veil of hullabaloo.

It's still there, you know.

Even when interruptions rip my best-laid plans from my hands and reduce my dreams to dust, the splendor of God's presence still flows around me like a golden flood. Beauty, goodness, and wonder still swirl and twirl in dances that—though unseen by human eyes—are sensed in the depths of our souls. There is still glory in the sea straining against the shoreline; there is still glory in the tumbling of a pinecone to the earth beneath a tree; there is still glory in every atom of oxygen that skips within my lungs. Simply put, *the glory goes on*.

This is a liberating truth. Through this truth I am freed from the unending lament, *What did I do to deserve this?* Certainly there are times when I must deal with the consequences of my actions, and there are moments when life is unfair. Yet these crosswinds cannot eclipse the truth that divine glory still waits for me beneath the veil of unexpected interruptions.

According to the apostle Paul, the "momentary affliction" we feel—the hullabaloo—"is producing for us an *eternal* weight of glory" (2 Cor. 4:17 NASB). In other words, amid the interruptions there is a glory here and now that will stretch out into eternity. "Is producing," Paul says—not "may someday produce." This present, eternal glory is the heavyweight stuff of life here and now. And, even in the shadow of the interruptions, this glory goes on.

I experienced it firsthand by spending Christmas with a dead man.

Christmas with a Dead Man

John was everything a pastor wants in a church member; he always laughed, he was always on time, and he always said "Amen" at the right moment during the sermon, except when something convicted him. Then he said, "Ouch."

It was around Thanksgiving when John learned from his doctor that his cancer had consumed any hopes he might have had for his future. John relayed the news to me in the form of a corny anecdote involving a Labrador retriever and a housecat performing a CAT scan and a lab report on him. I didn't know whether to laugh or to cry.

Before it was over, I did both.

He said he wanted to celebrate Christmas with his family.

A few days before Christmas John lay in his living room, unable to leave the white-sheeted hospital bed. I watched John's fingertips trace a line along his wife's forehead, gently yet hungrily, as if he longed to take this familiar texture with him into eternity. He told his wife that she was the most beautiful creature he had ever seen; then, he gripped the hands of their two daughters, whispered his love for them, and slipped into a fitful sleep.

"He will last until Christmas," I told my wife when I returned home. "And in case there comes a day when I don't have the chance to tell you, you are more beautiful in my eyes than you will ever know."

On December 25, late in the afternoon, John's eyes suddenly opened wide, as if his soul had glimpsed something that far outstripped his wildest imaginations. An instant later the heart monitor began to howl. When I reached the living room, John's wife and daughters were stroking his mouth and forehead with a damp cloth. The rhythmic rise and fall of his chest had ceased. Whatever the mysterious entity is that slips from the body at the end of life was gone.

And for a time, there was weeping, not hysterical howls of rage or regret, but the hushed murmurings of spirits that have been deeply bruised, the groaning of souls that still hope for a life beyond this one.

As we waited for the coroner to arrive, the sobs slowly faded, and something unexpected began to happen. Family members began to tell stories about John—joyful echoes of the life they had shared. Children began to nibble at the holiday dinner that had been heaped on the table. Then, a grandson tore open some Christmas presents. Soon I began to hear an occasional chuckle, mingling seamlessly with sniffles and sobs.

It should have seemed strange, celebrating Christmas with a dead man in the *living* room, no less. But it didn't. It seemed, somehow, as if this was the way life was supposed to be lived.

There was no hiding from the interruptions of life, no denying the reality of undeserved sickness, sorrow, and death.

Yet there was, at the same time, an unspoken awareness that no interruption—not even death—could completely eclipse the beauty, goodness, and wonder of life. Somehow they knew the glory goes on.

The Gift of Glory

When I live as if the glory goes on, unexpected interruptions will still jar my daily existence. Yet I live as if there is something, or more precisely, *someone* far greater than me at work even in the interruptions. This someone doesn't always tip the scales of the hullabaloo in the direction of my desires, but he does gently and persistently nudge my life toward the dream he so deeply desired when he crafted the garden and placed our first parents deep in its verdant valleys. And regardless of what interruptions may disrupt my dreams, his glory goes on.

What's more, even though God never guarantees what I put into life will determine what I get out of it, he does offer me the gift of himself, the gift that is the essence of what we call "heaven." And perhaps, at the secret heart of all my hopes and dreams, that gift is all I really wanted after all.

Eleven

Darkness: When the Hullabaloo Doesn't Turn Glorious

Since we are [God's] children, we will share his treasures.... But if we are to share his glory, we must also share his suffering.

—The Apostle Paul, Romans 8:17 NLT

This glory is not conspicuous. It is not glamorous.... When we look up the glory of Jesus we find—are we ever ready for this?—obscurity, rejection and humiliation, incomprehension and misapprehension, a sacrificial life and an obedient death: the bright presence of God backlighting what the world despises or ignores.

—Eugene Peterson, *Christ Plays in Ten Thousand Places*

As we learn to view our lives with the imagination of a child, we learn to see the extraordinary reality beneath the surface of ordinary events, the treasures beneath the trash, glorious realities amid what once seemed like rubbish. All of life becomes tinged with the splendor of God. Even if the events of life don't change, at least our perspective changes so that we begin to glimpse the glory.

Most of the time.

But not always—at least not as far as I can see.

Sometimes the hullabaloo never seems to turn glorious.

Despite our best childlike imaginations, there are moments when our finest expectations crumble to dust and the hullabaloo turns to darkness.

You imagine a miracle in the emergency room, but your next stop after the hospital isn't your home. It's the funeral home.

You've searched for divine splendor in your spouse, but your marriage is still falling apart.

You wait with childlike eagerness for the glorious moment when you will bring a newborn baby into the freshly painted bedroom, but the crib remains empty.

You've looked for glory in your life's ordinary events, but you still can't shake the deep darkness in your soul; the shadows of your past always seem to eclipse any splendor that may surround you in the present.

Where is God's glory in these moments?

Where is the splendor of God in your times of suffering and waiting, of unwelcome interruptions and pain?

Where is the life of glory when all that you can see is darkness?

The truth I'm about to tell you isn't popular, and it isn't easy.

But it *is* the truth.

Your darkness is filled with glory.

Yes, really.

There is glory in the pain you never wanted, there is glory in the interruptions that you never expected, and there is glory in your ceaseless waiting for God to answer your prayers. Even in the darkness, there is glory.

Killing the "Sugar-Crystal and Saccharine" Deity

There is glory in the darkness.

Why does this truth seem so difficult to accept?

Somehow, contemporary Christians have picked up the concept that God's glory is more present when we're skipping toward the kingdom of God on our own well-planned paths than when we find ourselves facedown in the darkness, cheeks streaked with the sorrow of our shattered dreams. A glorious life—we seem to think—is a life of constant happiness, a life in which all the bills are paid ahead and all the shadows are left behind.

Best-selling Christian self-help books reinforce this sort of thinking with pleasant aphorisms: "God wants to increase you financially. Even if you come from an extremely successful family, God still wants you to go further. Think increase. Think abundance. Think more than enough."[1]

I wonder how the apostle Paul would have responded to such thinking. I imagine him now, huddled over his scrolls in the flickering candlelight. Winter is approaching, and he has no coat (2 Tim. 4:9–21). Nearly two hundred lashes from a leather whip years ago have reduced his back to a cracking mass of crisscrossed scars. His face is grotesque, disfigured from the time when he was stoned and left for dead (2 Cor. 11:24–25). Long ago in what now seems like another life, he was the most promising Jewish scholar in the

Roman Empire. But now he shivers in the corner of a shadowed cell in the depths of an imperial dungeon. He clutches his feather-quill pen and leather pouch in his armpit, trying desperately to warm the ink. Finally, he plunges the quill's sharpened calamus into his leather pouch. Clenching the pen between quivering fingers, Paul scratches these words on his last scrap of precious papyrus:

> I have no regrets.... That's why I stick it out here—so that everyone God calls will get in on the salvation of Christ in all its glory.... Anyone who wants to live all out for Christ is in for a lot of trouble; there's no getting around it.... I'm about to die, my life an offering on God's altar. This is the only race worth running. I've run hard right to the finish, believed all the way. (2 Tim. 1:12; 2:10; 3:12; 4:6–7 MSG)

Years earlier Paul had described the relationship between suffering and glory in this way: "Since we are [God's] children, we will share his treasures.... But if we are to share his glory, we must also share his suffering" (Rom. 8:17 NLT). It sounded so poetic then, when he was encouraging the Roman Christians to remain strong. Now Paul is the one sharing in the sufferings of Jesus, and his poetry is mingled with pain.

Still, Paul's last letter ends with a note of glory: "The Lord will rescue me from every evil deed," the aged apostle declares as he watches death approaching, "and will bring me safely to His heavenly kingdom; to Him be the glory" (2 Tim. 4:18 NASB). Somehow I can't fathom that Paul's consuming passion as he penned these words in a Roman dungeon was, "Think increase. Think abundance. Think more than enough,"—not in any earthly sense anyway.

In the novel *Fahrenheit 451,* science-fiction writer Ray

Bradbury foresaw a day when the character of Jesus would become an entertainment icon who promotes commercial products, a tool to satisfy humanity's thirst for material wealth. After hearing the words of Jesus from a now-forbidden Bible, one character comments,

> Lord, how they've changed it in our "parlors" these days. I often wonder if God recognizes his own son the way we've dressed him up, or is it dressed him down? He's a regular peppermint stick now, all sugar-crystal and saccharine when he isn't making veiled references to certain commercial products that every worshiper *absolutely* needs.[2]

When we begin to believe God's purpose is to increase the ease of our present lives, we are not far from the "sugar-crystal and saccharine" deity that haunts Ray Bradbury's anti-utopian vision of the future.

This deity is a tempting substitute for the true God, to be sure, but a god of "sugar-crystal and saccharine" always falls short of authentic glory. What's worse, this idol lures us into the lie that our lives are supposed to be "all sugar-crystal and saccharine" too. When life turns bitter, we believe that the glory is gone. In truth, it is often in the moments when life turns bitter that the real glory has just begun.

Glory in the Darkness

The primary problem with the assumption that ease and glory go together is that the most glorious life ever lived—the life of

Jesus—was a life of interruptions and waiting, of poverty and pain. Remember what one of the prophets wrote after God gave him a glimpse of his future Messiah's life?

> The servant grew up before God—a scrawny seedling, a scrubby plant in a parched field. There was nothing attractive about him, nothing to cause us to take a second look. He was looked down on and passed over, a man who suffered, who knew pain firsthand. One look at him and people turned away. We looked down on him, thought he was scum. (Isa. 53:2–3 MSG)

Perhaps if Jesus had been born today, someone could have shown him some surefire steps to success so he could have lived his best life now. Then maybe he wouldn't have had to live as "a man of sorrows and acquainted with grief" (Isa. 53:3 NASB). Perhaps he could have even skipped the cross.

But what if Jesus acquainted himself with grief on purpose?

What if Jesus refused to avoid sorrow for a reason?

And what if—because the Lord of Glory has embraced your darkness and made it his own—even your darkness is full of glory (see 1 Cor. 2:8)?

"The fact is," Isaiah claimed, "it was our pains he carried—our disfigurements, all the things wrong with us" (Isa. 53:4 MSG). If I understand this passage correctly, what the prophet was saying is that through his life of sufferings, Jesus not only took the punishment for your sins but also became present in your pain. As a result, *your darkness is full of glory because your darkness is full of Jesus*.

That's why, when Jesus envisioned the dark moment when he would suffer the pain and shame of all creation, he was able to whisper, "The hour has come for the Son of Man to be *glorified"* (John 12:23). "He continually mentions 'glory,'" a fourth-century pastor named John Chrysostom commented, "precisely because his cross—something that seemed like a reproach—was drawing near."[3] Even after enduring death, Jesus said to some of his disciples, "Don't you see that these things had to happen, that the Messiah had to suffer and only then enter into his glory?" (Luke 24:26 MSG). Somehow Jesus was able to look even at his sufferings and see glory. He was able to look at his sufferings with the imagination of a child. And by emerging alive from the tomb three days later, he demonstrated that there is no darkness so deep that he cannot turn it into glory. It is for this reason that the dark side of the hullabaloo cannot be understood apart from Jesus. "From every angle," theologian Karl Barth once commented, "Jesus Christ is the key to the secret of creation," and he remains the key even in the darkness.[4]

And what, precisely, does glory look like in the darker circumstances of life?

It looks like the God of the Universe, refusing to avoid the groaning of his creation.

It looks like Jesus Christ, who had spent untold eternities experiencing nothing but the infinite beauty of being God, choosing to embrace your darkness and mine.

It looks like the beloved Son of God dangling from a cross.

On the cross, "[God] made Him who knew no sin to be sin" (2 Cor. 5:21 NASB). And that is the horrible paradox of the cross: On that Friday, the sinless one became the sinfulness of all sinners, the vile essence of sin itself. Walter Wangerin, Jr. writes that, in those moments, Jesus Christ

> becomes a bad man, the worst of all men, the badness, in fact, of all men and all women together … Between

> the third hour and the ninth hour, beneath a blackening sky, [he] becomes the rebellion of humankind against its God.... Yet [he] is also the Holy One of God ... Holy, he must hate sin with an unyielding hatred. Behold, then, and see a sorrow unlike any other sorrow in the universe: that right now Jesus hates himself with unyielding hatred.[5]

In this way God gains a ghastly new experience: Through the death of Jesus, God experiences sin. Not the experience of committing sin. Not the fleeting rush of false satisfaction seducing us into coming back for more. Not the feeble imitations of God's pleasure that the world foolishly calls pleasure. No, God experiences sin as it truly is: God experiences the decades of self-hatred that follow the fleeting rush of pleasure; God drinks down the dregs of addiction and exploitation; God freely endures the darkest groaning of a broken world. Whatever struggles fill the hullabaloo of your daily life, Jesus has endured already, and he carries the sorrow with you. Through his suffering Jesus has filled your waiting, your interruptions, your sorrow, and your pain with the gift of himself. Your suffering is his suffering, and his suffering is yours (see Rom. 8:17; Col. 1:24).

Your darkness is filled with glory because, on the cross, God filled your darkness with himself.

This is, I believe, the only adequate answer in the moments when the hullabaloo turns dark. It's an embarrassing answer, to be sure. After all, who else worships a deity who was senseless enough to get himself nailed to a cross? But only a God who has hung in just such a place can empathize with his people when their circumstances nail them to the stakes of loneliness, loss, abandonment, persecution, and abuse. Such a God knows how it feels to scream into the darkness, to live in sorrow, to be the victim. On the Hill of the Skull, he chose to fill your sorrows with himself.

God in the Darkness

Suppose you began to look at your moments of deepest frustration remembering that Jesus is present—not in some vague, symbolic sense, but truly and literally in your sorrows.

Perhaps as you waited for God to answer your prayers, you would remember the one who screamed into the silence of Gethsemane, "My Father! If it is possible, let this cup of suffering be taken away from me," and no one answered (Matt. 26:39 NLT; see also Heb. 5:7)—not immediately, anyway, and not audibly. In fact, as far as any human being could tell, heaven remained silent. And because the Lord of Glory endured the silence of heaven, your waiting is a distant echo of his waiting, and there is glory in the waiting.

Perhaps, as you struggle to rebuild a strained relationship with your spouse, you would see that God is present in your suffering. Consider the pain that rips at God's heart as he remembers the beauty he envisioned so long ago when Adam's hand first slid into Eve's. And now, in your relationship and in so many others, the glory of male and female, and with it the image of God, has been twisted into a mangled fragment of what God planned (Gen. 1:26–27). Your pain has become God's pain, and there is glory in the pain.

Perhaps in every interruption and every sorrow, in every pain and unanswered prayer, you would imagine the presence of the one who entered into your sufferings and made them his own.

And then, maybe you would begin to glimpse the faintest glimmers of glory in your life again.

What I'm suggesting isn't easy. However, as Karl Barth noted, "Humanity cannot … complain that God is requiring too much, … because what God required of himself on humanity's behalf is infinitely greater than anything that God has required of humanity."[6] In other words, looking for glory in the hullabaloo wasn't easy for Jesus either. In his life and in ours the glory doesn't always *feel* glorious. Eugene Peterson has observed,

> The glory with which Jesus was glorified and the glory for which Jesus prayed for us is quite different than the kinds of glory that we are conditioned to want and admire.
>
> This glory is not conspicuous. It is not glamorous. It is not the glory that gets featured in glossy magazines or travel posters. It is not a glory noticed by fashion editors. It is not a glory that flatters our lusts and egos.
>
> But it is no less glory for all that. This glory, once we perceive it, is the brightness radiating from God as he moves into our neighborhood.… Jesus is the dictionary in which we look up the meaning of words. When we look up the glory of Jesus we find—are we ever ready for this?—obscurity, rejection and humiliation, incomprehension and misapprehension, a sacrificial life and an obedient death: the bright presence of God backlighting what the world despises or ignores.[7]

Frankly, it's far easier to try to escape your frustrations than it is to look for Jesus in what the world despises and ignores.

It's easier to view your pains as inconveniences to be avoided and your struggles as problems you can solve if only you find the right prescriptive solution. But your life is not a problem to be fixed or a puzzle to be solved in a series of surefire steps. Your life is an unpredictable adventure meant to be lived to its fullest, infused with splendor by a Spirit that no human eye can see—even in your moments of darkness.

This sort of life is messy and unpredictable. It doesn't easily fit into any predetermined series of steps. It might even be the sort of life that could get someone nailed to a cross. And yet God has guaranteed that this sort of life is the life of glory. The apostle Paul put it this way:

> That is why we never give up.... For our present troubles are quite small and won't last very long. Yet they produce for us an immeasurably great glory that will last forever! So we don't look at the troubles we can see right now; rather, we look forward to what we have not yet seen. (2 Cor. 4:16–18 NLT)

Paul seems to think it's possible to gaze through the hullabaloo—"the troubles we can see right now"—and glimpse glorious possibilities.

If Paul's words are true, there is glory in your struggles and glory in your doubt; there is glory in the interruptions that you never saw coming and glory in your waiting for the promises you sensed so long ago. That's what children are able to imagine when they look at the ordinary objects and imagine supernatural events surrounding them, and that's why God's kingdom belongs to them. That's what God can enable you to see too.

It just takes a little imagination.

Okay, it takes a *lot* of imagination.

But as Jesus, someone who was well acquainted with grief, once commented, "With God all things are possible" (Matt. 19:26 NIV)—even an imagination that glimpses glory in the darkness.

Twelve

Trust: When I Cannot See His Face

God's school is not like most. It's not regimented, age-adjusted, fixed in its curricula. The classroom is life itself; the curriculum, all of life's demands and interruptions and tedium, its surprises and disappointments.

—Mark Buchanan, "Schedule, Interrupted"

In this you rejoice, even if now for a little while you have had to suffer various trials, so that the genuineness of your faith … may be found to result in praise and glory and honor when Jesus Christ is revealed. Although you have not seen him, you love him; and even though you do not see him now, you believe in him and rejoice with an indescribable and glorious joy, for you are receiving the outcome of your faith, the salvation of your souls.

—Peter the Apostle, 1 Peter 1:6-9

My eyes fluttered open, and my mind groped to find its place in the larger continuum of life. I knew something had changed in the past few days, but I couldn't recall *what*. Something momentous … life-changing … but …

Oh, yes.

She was here.

Here, in this house.

The morning before, a seven-year-old girl had struggled up our front steps, tattered vinyl suitcase clutched to her chest. In the room where we had wept so often for the baby that never came, I had worked with this child to arrange her meager possessions in dresser drawers and toy chests. Then we wandered to a nearby park where—for the first time in my life—I caught a child in my arms and heard her squeal with delight, "Daddy! Daddy!"

But was this really true?

Was this merely a dream that had somehow lingered in this moment when darkness and dawn flirted with one another along the eastern horizon?

I lay there for several minutes, straining to separate dreams from reality.

As soon as sunlight began to stream through the window, I sank my feet into the carpet and padded into the middle bedroom. I needed to know if this dream was real. I peeked around the corner into the bedroom, and a relieved sigh slipped through my teeth. In a bed that my father had built for me, a little girl slept, dark curls forming a silken halo around her face.

It *was* true.

This child really was residing under my roof.

I knelt beside the bed and slid my arm around the child's shoulders. As I drew Hannah close to me her body stiffened and her eyes flashed open. She looked wildly around the room and then stared into my face. Thus far in her brief life, she had lived with three different sets of parents in a half-dozen homes in two countries. At this moment she did not seem to be certain where she was or which parent it was that now held her.

"It's okay," I whispered. "It's your daddy. This is your new home. Remember? It's me."

Hannah nodded mutely, but her body stayed stiff and her eyes remained wide. Ever so gradually, she began to relax. Finally, she snuggled close to me and fell asleep in my arms.

I liked the way she felt in my arms, to tell you the truth—this little girl breathing ever so gently into my chest, her hair rippling across my shoulder and tickling my throat.

In this way a ritual began. Each morning I slipped into Hannah's room to hold her for a few moments. Each morning she awoke with a burst of confusion and fear. Then, slowly, she drew close to me and rested.

Our routine continued for nearly three months. Then, one Saturday morning in August, something happened.

I knelt beside Hannah's bed, gently pulled her body toward me, and her eyes did not open. At first, a burst of sheer terror chilled my stomach. *Was she okay?*

Then it happened.

Hannah settled herself into my arms and murmured softly, "I love you, Daddy." With this she returned to sleep. No opening of her eyes. No stiffening in her limbs. No frightened glances around the room. In place of the terror, there was trust. She knew my touch so well that she had settled into my embrace without even opening her eyes to make certain it was me.

She had learned to trust my hands even when she could not see my face.

That's how I long to trust my heavenly Father.

Amid the hubbub and the hullabaloo of my daily life, I do not always see my Father's face. I cannot always find clear confirmations that my Father is near. Dark veils of disappointments, doubts, interruptions, and pain seem to hide his nearness. Yet he is always working, filling every moment of life with his glory even in the moments when I cannot see his face.

The problem is that I don't always live as though it is true.

I want to, though.

I want to live as though infinite glory surrounds my soul, even when an endless tide of hullabaloo is all my eyes can see. Some morning I long to wake up so certain of my Father's love that I feel his glory pulsing through every part of my life, even if there are no tangible signs of his presence to be found. I want to trust my Father's hand even when I cannot see his face.

When I learn to trust my Father's hand, I will discern the glory of God in the earthy aroma of well-brewed coffee, in the soft sweetness of my wife's skin, even in the few moments of silence that descend upon me when I find myself gridlocked in morning traffic.

When I learn to trust my Father's hand, I will recognize without even thinking about it that the blueness of the sky this morning is no mere meteorological fluke. The sky is blue today because God is wild about the color blue, and at some point in eternity past, God lovingly crafted this specific shade of blue for this specific sky on this specific day.

When I learn to trust my Father's hand, I will sense the halo of heaven along the edge of every earthly thing.

When I learn to trust my Father's hand, I will live every moment of my life in glory.

This sort of life does not happen instantly. It cannot be reduced to catchy acrostics or preprogrammed prayers. "God's school is not like most," Mark Buchanan has commented. "It's not regimented, age-adjusted, fixed in its curricula. The classroom is life itself; the curriculum, all of life's demands and interruptions and tedium, its surprises and disappointments."[1] This sort of trust emerges slowly as I come to the full realization of the truth about divine glory: All the glory for which my soul is searching is hidden in the hullabaloo of the life I am already living.

That's the glory of the hullabaloo.

So I decided this
morning I would begin
looking for the glory in the hullabaloo.
So I walked outside before dawn,
tasting the beauty of planets and stars,
dancing in their wild ellipses around the sun.
And, God, there is so much glory around me every morning. I see Venus,
    glistering in the eastern sky, unearthly shades of orange and pink
    swirling along the horizon. The cat
    nuzzling my sandal-clad feet,
    mewing for his morning morsels of food.
And I suppose that's what I am doing too. I am
    nuzzling against your footstool, God,
    crying to you for what I need to live in your glory today.
It's an immense and beautiful image.
Until the cat bites my big toe.
Suddenly this reflection of deity
who otherwise would have blessed
the feline with an abundance of food
becomes wrathful
and decrees that the supplicant at his feet
shalt be punted over the back fence
to spend some quality time
with the neighbor's Doberman pinscher.

Then, I decide to show mercy instead.
I would like to think it's because I'm learning
to see the glory in the hullabaloo.
It's actually because I don't feel like chasing the cat
around the yard at five o'clock in the morning.
Especially when this cat will
always
eventually
win.
Oh well,
it's a start.
I guess.
I love you, Lord;
I'm beginning to glimpse glory all around me, all the time,
and I promise never to bite your big toe.
Now, if you'll excuse me, I need to go inside
and find a Band-Aid.
Amen.

Afterword

Please Get Rid of This Book

Near the beginning of the book, I claimed that everything you will ever need for a spiritual life is already available in the life that you're presently living. You don't need another conference, another curriculum, or another spiritual discipline. You don't even need this book.

I really meant that.

Now that you've finished this book, there's no need to keep it. After all, if the Spirit of God lives in you, you already have everything that you need to live a life of glory. Don't waste your time reading this book again, and don't set it on your shelf to collect dust. As long as this book rests on your shelf, you'll be tempted to look for God's glory within these pages. But this is not the place God's glory resides.

If you want to experience divine glory, don't look here.

Look more deeply into the Scriptures, into the lives of saints and sinners around you, and into the splendor of your present life. Those are the places where the story of God's glory is being written.

If you sincerely believe that the message in this book may help someone else, give it to that person. However, don't act as though this book has some mystical power to transform their lives. It's powerless to transform anyone's life. All that I possess is a deep longing to point out the glory already available in the life you are presently living.

If you don't know anyone on whom you want to inflict this book's message, take the book to a used bookstore and get some cash for it. Then, use those couple of dollars to purchase a kids' meal at a fast-food restaurant. Give the kids' meal to a homeless person (leave the toy in it!), and look for glory in the recipient's face.

If I have achieved my goal for this book, once you have

read it, you will no longer need it. So whatever you do, remember this: If I come to your house and see this book on your shelf, I will be very upset.

So, please, get rid of this book.

About the Author

For the past fourteen years, Timothy Paul Jones has served churches in Missouri and Oklahoma as a pastor and minister to students. In addition to bachelor's and master's degrees in biblical literature and pastoral ministry, he has earned a doctorate in educational leadership from the Southern Baptist Theological Seminary. Dr. Jones has served Midwestern Baptist Theological Seminary and Oklahoma Baptist University's Seminary Extension program as a visiting professor of biblical languages.

Dr. Jones is the author of *Christian History Made Easy*; *Prayers Jesus Prayed*; *Praying Like the Jew, Jesus*; *Finding God in a Galaxy Far, Far Away*; and *Answers to "The Da Vinci Code*." Nearly a half-million copies of his works are in print around the world. His articles have appeared in *Discipleship Journal, Religious Education*, *Christian Education Journal*, *Bibliotheca Sacra*, and *Midwestern Journal of Theology.* Dr. Jones has also contributed more than two hundred articles to two popular reference works, *Nelson's New Christian Dictionary* and *Nelson's Dictionary of Christianity,* and coauthored the Christian Booksellers Association "Top 50" best seller *The Da Vinci Codebreaker* with James L. Garlow.

Timothy Paul Jones has been married to his wife, Rayann, since 1994. In 2003 Rayann and Timothy became the adoptive parents of Hannah, a seven-year-old girl from Romania. They reside in Louisville, Kentucky, in a house owned by two cats, Shadowfax and Martin Luther, and a Siberian Husky named Remus Lupin. Hannah and her daddy spend their evenings playing *Star Wars* Miniatures and chasing each other around the house with lightsabers and Nerf guns. For more information about Dr. Timothy Paul Jones, visit http://www.timothypauljones.com.

Acknowledgments

I need to make a confession. My church doesn't have a confessional booth, so I'll make the confession here: All the personal anecdotes that I've told are true. Yet there have been times when, for the sake of the narrative flow, I've combined events that occurred separately. Or I have used outward actions and dialogue to represent inward thought processes. Several editors have assured me that every author does this, and I suppose they're correct. Still, at a time when the point of demarcation between fiction and fact is increasingly difficult to find, it's important to me that I'm completely honest.

My confession is hereby ended.

Two weeks before I finished this book, I devoured a text that's now one of my favorite books—right behind Ray Bradbury's *Fahrenheit 451* and Karl Barth's *Church Dogmatics.* It was *Christ Plays in Ten Thousand Places: A Conversation in Spiritual Theology* by Eugene Peterson. What amazed me as I read his book was the similarity between some of his ideas and the thoughts I had already written in *Hullabaloo*—and he, unlike me, is a respectable writer. I don't want to besmirch Dr. Peterson's reputation by linking his name with the ramblings in these pages, but *Christ Plays in Ten Thousand Places* did significantly influence the final form of this book.

I wrote this book at Panera Bread Company on Aspen Drive in Broken Arrow, Oklahoma, and at Jim Misch's splendid new Starbucks on 61st Street in Tulsa. The primary sustenance for this project has been the Venti Iced Coffee with two shots of peppermint flavoring. Thanks to a host of Starbucks baristas for getting it right. (Toshiba Satellite Notebook computers are able, by the way, to survive the spillage of a Venti Iced Coffee directly into the keyboard.) When I was struggling to complete a troublesome chapter, there was no cuisine more inspiring than the espresso gelato affogato at Nordaggio's on the Riverwalk in Jenks, Oklahoma.

My listening companions on this journey have been U2, John Coltrane, Bob Dylan, John Mayer, the Rolling Stones, Rich Mullins, and Garrison Keillor's *A Prairie Home Companion*. I've created a musical playlist to complement each chapter of this book. You can download the playlists by going to my Web site, http://www.timothypauljones.com and clicking the "Hullabaloo" link.

The companions of my heart on this journey have been my wife, Rayann, and our daughter, Hannah. At this point I no longer possess the words to describe how I feel. Through the two of you God has poured more glory into my life than I am capable of expressing in the frail words of human language. It is my hope that as you read these pages, you will glimpse the glory I see in the two of you.

A couple of years ago, my mom said to me, "Write down the pain and the joy you felt as you went through the adoption process. It will help in your healing—and maybe it will help someone else." I did what she said, and much of what I wrote has found its way into this book. Thanks, Mom and Dad, for pressing me to write, even through the tears.

Thanks to Jeff Dunn, Diane Gardner, Emily Garman, and the other fine folk at Cook Communications for patience and encouragement throughout this project. You are an outstanding team, and I am privileged to work with you. Thanks to Mark Riddle, Greg Taylor, Laura Franklin, and Deby Nottingham for your comments on the early drafts of this manuscript. Special thanks to Mike Nappa at Nappaland Literary Agency for envisioning this project in the first place; I hope what you find here contains some small echo of your original dream. And thanks for including me in your newest venture!

Finally, I thank you, the reader. You've spent several hours of your life with me. I do not take your time or money lightly. I pray that you are more aware of God's presence now than you were when your journey through this book began. If I have offended or misled you in any way, please forgive me.

As I wrote this book, I assumed its readers would be followers of Jesus. If you are not certain whether you fit into that category, consider this an invitation to entrust your life to the risen Lord whose glory is available to you even here, even now.

Still learning to be God's child,
Timothy Paul Jones
Pentecost 2006

READERS' GUIDE

FOR PERSONAL REFLECTION OR GROUP STUDY

At some point in the pages that precede this one, I made this claim: "No product that you can purchase at your local bookstore and no program that your church will ever provide can possibly fill your life with the glory for which you were created. You don't need another conference, another curriculum, or another spiritual discipline." With words such as these ringing in my ears, it actually feels a bit hypocritical to include a readers' guide in this book.

That's why this guide will be unlike any readers' guide you've ever read.

This guide will not help you to start a small group in which you will have happy discussions about how to make your lives easier. Such groups aren't necessarily bad. I believe, however, that their capacity for lasting transformation has been highly overrated, while their capacity for breeding self-centeredness and discord has been underrated. At the same time I do believe that it is in the context of fellowship that we learn to experience glory in the hullabaloo, and small groups are a valuable form of faith-refining fellowship.

One

Emptiness: The Empty Field That Wasn't Empty After All

The music playlist for this chapter is available at the author's Web site, http://www.timothypauljones.com.

As an individual or in a small group, spend some time carefully studying the following Scriptures:

Job 1:1—3:26

Jeremiah 50:2–7

John 17:1–24

If you participate in a small group, go to a park or to an empty field together. Look for signs of life that aren't immediately visible. As you kneel or crawl on the ground, praise God aloud for each sign of life that you see. Afterward, share a picnic dinner. Conclude the dinner by celebrating the Lord's Supper together.

Two

Glory: When Your Messiah Drives a Minivan

The music playlist for this chapter is available at the author's Web site, http://www.timothypauljones.com.

As an individual or in a small group spend some time carefully studying the following Scriptures:

Acts 17:16–31

1 Thessalonians 2:11–12; 2 Thessalonians 2:14; 1 Peter 5:10

Romans 1:20–23; 3:23

If you participate in a small group, go to a mall or shopping center, but determine beforehand that you will not buy anything. Your sole goal is to glimpse divine glory in the people around you. Afterward, ask yourself, "On any given day, how much would I have spent on things that I don't really need?"

Later, meet with your small group at a restaurant. Before you pray, ask your server if there's any area of his or her life that needs prayer. After your meal, put together all the money that you would have spent on unneeded items and leave your server a disproportionately large tip with a note that reads something like this: "God created you to live in his glory. We pray you will experience that glory during this week."

THREE

HULLABALOO: LEARNING THE ART OF LIFE

The music playlist for this chapter is available at the author's Web site, http://www.timothypauljones.com.

As an individual or in a small group, spend some time carefully studying the following Scriptures:

2 Corinthians 4:13–18

Matthew 13:1–46

Luke 17:20–21

If you participate in a small group, read Matthew 13:31–43 together. Next, make plans to do one or both of the following projects together:

Plant several seeds in small flowerpots.

Make homemade yeast bread, mixing and kneading it by hand.

As you work on these projects, acknowledge that these ordinary activities can be sacramental events, acts of worship to God. Plan to take the fruits of your labor—whether fresh-baked bread or small seedlings—to several elderly persons. Ask each elderly person, "What has been the most glorious thing God has done in your life?" Then, simply listen, looking for glory in the stories this person tells.

Four

More: Why Nothing at the Convenience Store Can Satisfy Your Hunger

The music playlist for this chapter is available at the author's Web site, http://www.timothypauljones.com.

As an individual or in a small group, spend some time carefully studying the following Scriptures:

Deuteronomy 28:64–67

Ecclesiastes 3:1–11

Romans 8:18–23

If you participate in a small group, issue this challenge to one another: To help you to see how many things you buy to satisfy your longing for "more," begin this week with a ten-dollar bill in your billfold or purse. Try to go the entire week without purchasing a single item you do not need. If you do purchase something you don't need, you must use your ten-dollar bill. At your next gathering, allow people to share what they learned from this experience. If someone has spent some or all of his or her ten dollars, do not criticize the person; simply talk about what you each learned. After your meeting, go to a grocery store and use the money that remains from these ten-dollar bills to help pay for the groceries of strangers. If someone asks you why you're doing this, simply say something like, "Jesus Christ is desperately in love with you, and his glory surrounds you in every moment of your life. I want to share his glory with you."

Five

The Real You: Where God's Glory Lives Today—and Where It Doesn't

The music playlist for this chapter is available at the author's Web site, http://www.timothypauljones.com.

As an individual or in a small group, spend some time carefully studying the following Scriptures:

Luke 9:23–36

John 17:1, 20–26

Colossians 3:1–4

If you participate in a small group, write a letter to each group member, describing how glorious you believe he or she looks from God's perspective. Also, ask yourself, *How does God see this person? What does "the real me" look like in this person's life?* When you gather together, exchange letters. Read them silently. These letters aren't public communiqués; they are private epistles from one believer to another. After you have all had time to read your letters, spend some time praying together in complete silence. In the silence, envision each person as God sees him or her.

Six

Imagination: Why Children Hold the Title Deed to God's Kingdom

The music playlist for this chapter is available at the author's Web site, http://www.timothypauljones.com.

As an individual or in a small group, spend some time carefully studying the following Scriptures:

Matthew 18:1–10

Matthew 19:13–15

1 Corinthians 1:26–31

If you participate in a small group, volunteer together to participate in your church's children's ministry by teaching a lesson. As you interact with the children, pay close attention to how they see glory where the rest of the world sees garbage. As a class, write notes to the parents of each child, describing what you learned from their children.

Seven

Control: Why You Still Stink at Following Jesus

The music playlist for this chapter is available at the author's Web site, http://www.timothypauljones.com.

As an individual or in a small group, spend some time carefully studying the following Scriptures:

Matthew 5:21–26

James 1:17–21

Romans 1:18–23

1 Thessalonians 5:18

If you participate in a small group, encourage everyone to keep a journal throughout the week, noting each time they become aware of cravings for control in their life. Before your next gathering, spend twenty-four hours fasting. Fasting is, after all, a release of our longing to be in control of our food. When you meet again, spend your entire time together in prayer, thanking God for each present moment of life.

Eight

Together: The Trouble with Human Beings

The music playlist for this chapter is available at the author's Web site, http://www.timothypauljones.com.

As an individual or in a small group spend some time carefully studying the following Scriptures:

Genesis 1:26–31

Mark 3:13–15

Hebrews 11:39—12:1

As you meditate on Hebrews 12:1, choose a song from the playlist and play air guitar with one of the saints of the past. Okay, so maybe you really don't need to play air guitar with the saints. The point is to engage in some activity that consciously recognizes that the saints of the past are still present with us today. Perhaps you could collect and read aloud the writings of a past saint and consider the fact that, according to Hebrews 12:1–2, this saint is still present in the fellowship of God's people. To conclude your meeting, gather together to take the Lord's Supper and meditate on the fact that the saints of the past gather with you. Or play air guitar.

Nine

Interruptions: Why Bad Karma Isn't Necessarily a Bad Thing

The music playlist for this chapter is available at the author's Web site, http://www.timothypauljones.com.

As an individual or in a small group, spend some time carefully studying the following Scriptures:

John 9:1–41

Ecclesiastes 11:1–6

Proverbs 14:11; 16:3; 22:3

After reading the verses from the book of Proverbs, consider that some people may believe that life in God operates according to cause-and-effect sequences. Some proverbs seem to imply that what you put into life dictates exactly what you get out of it. What's easy to miss, however, is the fact that proverbs are not promises. The proverbial passages in Scripture are observations about how the hullabaloo usually works; they are inspired wisdom, tested by time. But they are not promises, and they do not guarantee that what you put into life determines what you get out of it.

If you participate in a small group, read together *How to Read Proverbs* by Tremper Longman III, especially pages 79–88.[1] Confess to one another concerning the times you have become frustrated with God because your life did not proceed in the cause-and-effect sequences you expected. Afterwards, do something that turns cause-and-effect sequences upside down: Together, demonstrate love and kindness to someone who may not believe that he or she deserves a glorious life.

Ten

Unfairness: Living as Though the Glory Goes On

The music playlist for this chapter is available at http://www.timothypauljones.com.

As an individual or in a small group, spend some time carefully studying the following Scriptures:

Ecclesiastes 2:20–23; 6:1–2

Job 1—5; 8:1–22; 13:1–28; 19:1–29; 29:1–25; 38—42

If you participate in a small group, visit a nursing home together—preferably a low-income care center. Pray with as many residents as possible. Between your times of prayer, ask God to help you to see that many of these people deserve something far better than their present situation. For most of them, life is unfair. (Approximately 60 percent of persons in extended care centers never have a single visitor. Visit http://www.therubins.com/homes/stathome.htm. You cannot make life "fair," but you can be a source of God's glory to people whom others have forgotten.)

Eleven

Darkness: When the Hullabaloo Doesn't Turn Glorious

The music playlist for this chapter is available at the author's Web site, http://www.timothypauljones.com.

As an individual or in a small group, spend some time carefully studying the following Scriptures:

2 Timothy 1—4, keeping in mind Paul's circumstances as he wrote this letter

Romans 8:15–17

Isaiah 53:1–12

If you participate in a small group, think of someone who recently experienced a personal tragedy. Together, make plans to become an expression of divine glory to this person or family. Keep their lawn mowed for a month or two; invite them somewhere for dinner at least once each week; or leave a gift card for gasoline or food on their door—whatever God leads you to do. But do not, under any circumstances, try to explain why this tragedy has happened. Simply *be* the glory of God in this person's life.

TWELVE

Trust: When I Cannot See His Face

The music playlist for this chapter is available at the author's Web site, http://www.timothypauljones.com.

As an individual or in a small group, spend some time carefully studying the following Scriptures:

1 Peter 1:3–9

Hebrews 11:1–2

If you participate in a small group, read together the section titled "Afterword: Please Get Rid of This Book." As a group, plan how you will get rid of your copies of this book in constructive yet enjoyable ways.

NOTES

Introduction

1. H. F. W. Gesenius, S. R. Driver, and Charles A. Briggs, *A Hebrew and English Lexicon of the Old Testament,* ed. Frances Brown and trans. Edward Robinson (Oxford: Oxford University Press, 1952), 457–459.

Chapter 1

1. Language alludes to Frederick Buechner, *Wishful Thinking: A Seeker's ABC* (New York: HarperSanFrancisco, 1993), 2.
2. See, for example, John Bunyan, *The Pilgrim's Progress* (Mineola, NY: Dover Publications, 2003).
3. C. S. Lewis, *Perelandra: A Novel* (New York: Scribner, 1943), 81.
4. C. S. Lewis, "The Weight of Glory," in *The Weight of Glory: And Other Addresses* (New York: MacMillan, 1949), 11.
5. Huston Smith, *The Soul of Christianity: Restoring the Great Tradition* (New York: HarperSanFrancisco, 2005), xii.
6. U2, "God, Part II," *Rattle and Hum*, Island Records, compact disc, B000001FS6.
7. Most commentaries on this text see little more in the text than the fact that, by abandoning the God to whom they belonged, the Israelites also abandoned any sense of security. J. A. Thompson's analysis is typical: "They forgot … the place where they were cared for and nurtured by Yahweh their true shepherd.… [Israel] had sinned (*hata*) against him who was her *true pasture.*" (*The Book of Jeremiah* [Grand Rapids: Eerdmans, 1980], 733). Yet it seems that there must be some deeper reason for such a unique metaphor for God.
8. Walter Hooper, "C. S. Lewis: Literary Chameleon," in *Behind the Veil of Familiarity,* eds. M. C. Gonzalez and E. H. Tenorio (Bern, Switzerland: Peter Lang, 2001), 25.

Chapter 2

1. The glory of God is objective, separate from and external to individual human beings; the experience of glory, on the other hand, is subjective and existential, occurring within the individual—even within the pre-Christian individual, though she or he may misinterpret or deny the true source of this experience (cf. Rom. 1:19–23). At its best,

Christian spirituality seeks a point at which the objective reality and the subjective experience coincide.

2. The experience that I have referred to as "glory" has also been described as "the awareness of utter dependence" (*das schlechthinnigen Abhängigkeitsgefuehl*), "spiritual transcendence," and "relational consciousness"; it is similar to—though less intensive than—Rudolf Otto's "mystery that fascinates and terrifies" (*mysterium fascinans et tremendum*). See D. Hay and R. Nye, *Spirit of the Child* (Loveland, CO: Fount, 1998), 10; T. Jones, "Fowler's Stages of Faith and Schleiermacher's *Gefuehl* as Spiritual Transcendence," *Midwestern Journal of Theology* (Spring 2005): 59–71; Rudolf Otto, *Das Heilige* (Breslau, Poland: Trewendt und Granier, 1923), 13–14; R. L. Piedmont, "Does Spirituality Represent the Sixth Factor of Personality?" *Journal of Personality* 67 (1999): 986–988; F. D. E. Schleiermacher, *Die christliche Sitte nach den Grundsätzen der evangelischen Kirche im Zusammenhang dargestellt* (Berlin: Reimer, 1843), 3:3; 5:1–3; 33:1; 34:1.
3. Eugene Peterson, *Christ Plays in Ten Thousand Places: A Conversation in Spiritual Theology* (Grand Rapids: Eerdmans, 2005), 103.
4. Lewis, *Perelandra,* 215.
5. Clause alludes to Susan E. Schreiner, *The Theater of His Glory: Nature and the Natural Order in the Thought of John Calvin*, Studies in Historical Theology (Durham, NC: Labyrinth Press, 1991).
6. Garrison Keillor, "On the Meaning of Life," in *We Are Still Married* (New York: Viking, 1989), as quoted in Tim Dearborn, *Taste and See: Awakening Our Spiritual Senses* (Downers Grove, IL: InterVarsity, 1996), 71.
7. Virginia Stem Owens, *And the Trees Clap Their Hands: Faith, Perception, and the New Physics* (Grand Rapids: Eerdmans, 1983).

Chapter 3

1. *Online Etymology Dictionary*, s.v., "Hullabaloo," http://www.etymonline.com/index.php?term=hullabaloo (accessed January 24, 2007).
2. C. S. Lewis, *The Voyage of the Dawn Treader,* The Chronicles of Narnia (New York: HarperCollins, 1994), 226.

3. Malcolm Muggeridge, "News Summaries," December 31, 1978, as quoted in Ken Gire, "Faithful Companions and Guides: Art and Nature as God's Chosen Vocabulary," *Mars Hill Review* (Fall 1996): 8–20.
4. Leonard Sweet, *Out of the Question—Into the Mystery: Getting Lost in the GodLife Relationship* (Colorado Springs: WaterBrook Press, 2004), 199.
5. G. K. Chesterton, "A Defense against Defending Things," Imaginarium Online, http://www.cornerstonemag.com/imaginarium/inklinks/ (accessed March 31, 2007).

Chapter 4

1. Craig Wiseman, Jeffrey Steele, and Al Anderson, "Cowboy in Me," as performed by Tim McGraw, *Set This Circus Down,* prod. Tim McGraw, Byron Gallimore, and James Stroud, Curb Special Markets compact disc 78711.
2. A. W. Tozer, *Knowledge of the Holy* (New York: Harper, 1961), 17.
3. Peterson, 102.
4. Brennan Manning, *The Ragamuffin Gospel* (Sisters, OR: Multnomah, 2000), 88–89.
5. Language alludes to Lewis, "The Weight of Glory," 31.
6. Donald Miller, *Through Painted Deserts: Light, God, and Beauty on the Open Road* (Nashville: Thomas Nelson, 2005), 10–11.
7. Descriptions allude to Stephen Covey, *Seven Habits of Highly Effective People* (New York: Simon and Schuster, 1989); Joel Osteen, *Your Best Life Now* (New York: Warner Faith, 2004); and, Rick Warren, *The Purpose-Driven Life* (Grand Rapids: Zondervan, 2002). My allusions to *The Purpose-Driven Life* and *Seven Habits of Highly Effective People* are not intended to reflect negative opinions of the books themselves. In fact, I have found many of Covey's time-management ideas to be helpful, and I have served in a church that profitably used Warren's book. What I view as a misappropriation of such books is the attitude that this curriculum—or any other—provides the consummate solution for the problems of a church or an individual. This is not, however, the fault of the book or its author; it is, rather, evidence of the contemporary church's widespread accommodation of consumerist mentalities

in its discipleship methods. Though I am certain Osteen's intentions are commendable, I do find *Your Best Life Now* to represent a precarious and highly selective approach to the text of Scripture.

Chapter 5

1. Charles Darwin, *The Descent of Man, and Selection in Relation to Sex* (London: J. Murray, 1871), 820, 827.
2. The original Greek text does not include any direct equivalent of Eugene Peterson's phrase "the real you." The text literally reads *"hotan ho Christos phanerothe he zoe hemon tote kai hymeis sun auto phanerothesesthe en doxe"* or "When the Messiah manifests himself (this is the one who is our life) at that time, even you—with him—will be manifested in glory." The clause "the one who is our life" implies the idea Peterson expresses so memorably in *The Message*—the true essence of our lives ("the real you") is to be found in the glory of Jesus Christ.

Chapter 6

1. Here, I have chosen to represent *elpis*—the Greek word typically translated "hope" in Colossians 1:27—with the English word *assurance*. Another rendering that would more accurately represent the original intent of the Greek *elpis* would be "present expectation."
2. This interpretation has a long history, with some of the church fathers—influenced by Platonism—even claiming that Jesus' central point was not the *innocence* of children but their *chastity*. See Hilary of Poitiers, "In Matthaeum," in *Sources chretiennes,* ed. H. de Lubac et al. (Paris: Editions du Cerf, 1941), 18:1, and Epiphanius the Latin, "Interpretatio Evangelorium," in *Patrilogiae Latinae Supplementum,* ed. A. Hamman (Paris: Garnier Freres, 1958), 3:862, 866–67.
3. Benjamin Nicholas et al., s.v. "patria potestas," in *The Oxford Classical Dictionary*, eds. Simon Hornblower and Anthony Spawforth (Oxford: Oxford University Press, 1996), 1122–123. For evidence that Jesus' words did not—in their social and cultural context—imply the innocence or purity of children, see Joachim Jeremias, *New Testament Theology* (New York: Scribners, 1971), 155–56; Joachim Jeremias, *The Parables of Jesus* (New York: Scribners, 1972), 190.

4. For this sense of "unless you become as children," see Brad H. Young, *Jesus the Jewish Theologian* (Peabody, MA: Hendrickson, 1995), 99.
5. Buechner, *Wishful Thinking,* 15.
6. Peterson, 123.
7. G. K. Chesterton, *Orthodoxy*, Abbaci Books, http://www.abacci.com/msreader/etext94/Orthodoxy.lit (accessed March 31, 2007).
8. Mark Buchanan, "Jesus Wept," *Christianity Today,* March 5, 2001, 68.

Chapter 7

1. For the source of this analogy, see William Law, *Liberal and Mystical Writings of William Law* (New York: Longmans, Green, 1908), 55.
2. Translated from John Calvin, *Institutio Christianae religionis,* in *Ioannis Calvini opera selecta* (Munich: Christliche Kaiser, 1926), 1:11:8.
3. Stanislav Grof contends fear is the first emotion that an infant experiences; it seems this fear and the frustration that follows may stem from the infant's initial recognition that she or he is not in control of her or his environment. See Stanislav Grof, *Spiritual Emergency: When Personal Transformation Becomes a Crisis* (New York: Putnam, 1989), 8–12.
4. Peterson, 52.
5. According to *The World Factbook*, 56,597,034 people die each year, meaning that approximately 155,060 persons die each day. See https://www.cia.gov/cia/publications/factbook/geos/xx.html#People (accessed March 31, 2007).
6. Myron Augsburger, "The Redeemed Community in a Fallen World," 30 Good Minutes, November 19, 1989, http://www.30goodminutes.org/csec/sermon/augsburger_3308.htm (accessed March 31, 2007).
7. Henri Nouwen, *The Return of the Prodigal Son: A Story of Homecoming* (New York: Image, 1992), 85–86.

Chapter 8

1. Early theologians of the Eastern Orthodox Church—especially John of Damascus—used *perichoresis* to describe the relationships of Father, Son, and Spirit within the Trinity. This term means "to

interpenetrate" or "to dance around one another." It is from this background that I derive the descriptive language of Father, Son, and Spirit dancing. See Verna Harrison, "Perichoresis in the Greek Fathers," *St. Vladimir's Theological Quarterly* 35 (1991): 61; Michael G. Lawler, "Perichoresis," *Horizons* 22 (Spring 1995): 52; Vladimir Lossky, *The Mystical Theology of the Eastern Church* (Crestwood, NY: St. Vladimir's, 1976), 52–54.

2. William Willimon and Stanley Hauerwas, *Lord, Teach Us* (Nashville: Abingdon, 1996), 28, 29, 77, 108.
3. James Bryan Smith, *Rich Mullins: An Arrow Pointing to Heaven* (Nashville: Broadman and Holman, 2000), 45.
4. C. S. Lewis, *Surprised by Joy* (New York: Harcourt, 1955), 228–229.

Chapter 9

1. Robert Burns, "To a Mouse," in *Poetical Works of Robert Burns* (London: Kessinger, 2003), 28–29.
2. The Hebrew prophets clearly affirm that there are times when tragedies signify divine discipline (see, for examples, Isa. 1—5; Jer. 13:20–23; 14:10). This perspective is, however, balanced by Job and Ecclesiastes where it is clear that tragedies happen not only to unrighteous people but also to the righteous.
3. H. L. Strack and P. Billerbeck, *Kommentar zum neuen Testament aus Talmud und Midrasch*, vol. 2 (Muenchen, Germany: C.H. Beck, 1926–1961), 527–529.
4. D. A. Carson, *The Gospel According to John: An Introduction and Commentary* (Grand Rapids: Eerdmans, 1991), 361–362.
5. Language alludes to Mark Buchanan, "Schedule, Interrupted: Discovering God's Time-Management," *Christianity Today*, February 1, 2006, http://www.christianitytoday.com/ct/2006/002/29.43.html (accessed March 31, 2007).

Chapter 10

1. William Goldman, *The Princess Bride: S. Morgenstern's Classic Tale of True Love and High Adventure* (New York: Del Rey, 1987), 206–208, 315.
2. Refers to the scientific phenomenon of "sensitivity to initial

conditions," commonly known as "the butterfly effect." See E. N. Lorenz, "Deterministic Nonperiodic Flow," *Journal of Atmospheric Science* 357 (1963): 130–141.

3. C. S. Lewis, *Letters to Malcolm: Chiefly on Prayer* (New York: Harcourt, Brace, Jovanovich, 1964), 75.

Chapter 11

1. Osteen, 5, 9, 11.
2. Ray Bradbury, *Fahrenheit 451* (New York: Del Rey, 1987), 81.
3. Translated from John Chrysostom, *"Homilae in Matthaeum,"* in *Patrilogiae cursus completus: Series Graeca,* ed. J.-P. Migne (Paris: Migne, 1854), 58:717.
4. Translated from Karl Barth, *Die kirchliche Dogmatik* (Zurich, Switzerland: Evangelische Verlag, 1936–1962), 2:2:166.
5. Walter Wangerin, Jr., *Reliving the Passion* (Grand Rapids: Zondervan, 1992), 121–123.
6. Barth, 3:1:28.
7. Peterson, 103.

Chapter 12

1. Mark Buchanan, "Schedule, Interrupted."

Readers' Guide

1. Tremper Longman III, *How to Read Proverbs* (Downers Grove, IL: InterVarsity Press, 2002), 79–88. See also Raymond van Leeuwen, "Wealth and Poverty: System and Contradiction in Proverbs," *Hebrew Studies* 33 (1992): 25–36; Bruce Waltke, "Does Proverbs Promise Too Much?" *Andrews University Seminary Studies* 34 (1996): 319–326.